36 HOURS TO LIVE:
The diary of a disheartened Teen

By
Tom Gnagey

Loosely based on a teen boy's very personal diary.

Family of Man Press

© 2019

Republished
with editing and reorganization
from the original publication in 1994.

[To those who have previously read, **And Then Came *Arnie,*** a chronical of the year the primary character in this story was nine years old:
You may notice some disconnect between that account and this one. It has been the author's intent to present the essence of both stories in a readable and meaningful way rather than as a continuous chronical. In certain instances, it was necessary to augment or otherwise modify certain elements in the boy's life.]

Dedication

To
Young people everywhere,
who may now be questioning the
value of
their own life,
and
to the memory of those,
now gone,
who gave up their search
prematurely

- TDG

Things you will want to know
as you begin

You are about to begin reading the diary of 16-year-old Craig Franklin. It contains the most personal, private, and cherished thoughts of a sad and desperate sixteen-year-old boy. Being allowed this look into Craig's mind, is a very special privilege. As you will soon see, Craig wanted to share these thoughts with you, so you might learn from them and use them to form a clearer understanding of - not him, so much - but of yourself.

His plan was clear. It was carefully and thoughtfully designed to make this diary a summary of his life: his ideas, dreams, hopes, unresolved questions and conflicts, emotions, regrets, highs and lows, and, of his final advice to you on how to live the good life as he had come to define it.

In his diary, Craig carefully chronicled, in ritualistic, hour by hour fashion, what he had planned would be his final thirty-six hours. The year, as you will soon understand, is unimportant, since his message is timeless.

In several ways, Craig was, indeed, different from most young people. He was born a genius - for better or for worse - you may decide that for yourself. At age two, he was orphaned and then raised by a poor, elderly, childless couple in the small town of Springfield. Because of these two situations, the course of Craig's life was obviously different from that of most children.

As the details of his life unfold in the pages that follow, you will come to understand that in most other ways, Craig was a very typical youngster. He had the same dreams and fears as most kids. He wanted to be safe, popular, athletic, good looking, and accepted by his peers. As he matured, he wanted girls to like him, and boys to respect his strength and physical skills.

While he was generally a loving and well-behaved young man, Craig had disagreements with his parents, got grounded, and frequently felt totally misunderstood by every last person on Earth! He wondered why adults seem to so easily forget how it really was to be an adolescent. He feared rejection by his age mates and occasionally did things, which were really against his own values in order to be one of the group.

When Craig was in love (which was often!), he was on cloud nine! When he broke up, (equally as often), his world was truly shattered.

Now, since Craig was so typical in so many ways, some of the normal, sixteen-year-old male thoughts recorded here are somewhat graphic, explicit, irreverent, and occasionally, vulgar, perhaps. They are, however, always honest and open and sincere - more honest and open, I believe, than most adolescents could be, knowing that others might be reading them someday. It is my sincere hope that you can set aside any tendency to feel offended or embarrassed by such passages. Just allow yourself to absorb and grapple with the bigger picture - the over-all theme - a real sixteen-year-old, engaged in the ultimate struggle, as he tries to make sense out of life and of the processes of living and dying.

The author has assembled this book primarily for readers beyond the age of thirteen. He has, of course, no control over who may read it. So, especially to the younger reader, he makes this plea: As you come across material that you do not understand or that is frightening or bothersome to you, please, talk it over with an adult you respect and trust. Keep in mind that life is precious, and that *that* is, really, what this book is about.

In many ways, Craig was wise beyond his years, but don't expect his commentaries to all be accurate or his charges against society and social institutions to all be fully legitimate.

As you read through these pages for the first time, try not to argue points with him in your mind. Just try to understand him, absorb his words, feel his emotions, enjoy his wit, appreciate his sincerity, and let him reach out through time and touch you - one friend to another - just as he hoped he could.

I do need your word on one thing: if you begin the book, you must finish it. The message is not complete, not truly useful unless you have read and understood every single word. Thank you for that.

/

The Final Diary
of
Craig Franklin

11:00 AM
July 4, 1952

Dear Diary,
It's amazing! It's like magic! It's unbelievable! But once I finally made the decision to do it, all my fears just vanished; all my tensions left; all my uncertainties ceased. I truly haven't felt this good - no, this absolutely terrific - in, well, maybe ever.

I don't have to be concerned about pleasing Mom, or getting a date, or figuring out what to be. I'm no longer worrying about how I look, my complexion, being poor, being small for my class, pleasing Mr. Elzer at the grocery store, disappointing myself and others.

What a fantastically free feeling this is! It's like soaring above the crowd. I want to just shout at everyone, "Why don't you see it, too? End your misery! Put your tortured minds at peace. Follow me! Who says you have to just keep trying? Who says you have to go on? How simple! How sensible! How easy!"

I learned long ago that no one listens when you yell at them, so instead, I'm going to write it all here, to you, Di. I wonder when I started calling you, "Di," instead of Diary. A long, long time ago. I guess I never asked your permission. Hope you haven't minded. (smile)

You've been my best friend and confidant since I first learned how to write. When was that - about four, I guess? I've chronicled my everyday here in your pages. How many, many, volumes must there be by now? I've shared with you my deepest thoughts, confessed my gravest sins, grappled here with the mysteries of the universe, and amused you (or at least myself!) with my silliest and most absurd commentaries on everything from god to lint.

You know, Di, how hard I have worked to improve my writing skills, so one day I could write that very special book - the one that would reach deep down inside everyone who read it and change their lives forever. Well, I guess this must be it! At least it's going to be my last chance.

Remember when I used to show some parts of my diary to Mrs. Heatherton at school? She'd say, "Craig, you sound like an old man in here - Ease up - Free your thoughts from proper writing form. Just let it flow. It's a diary - not your last will and testament!" Well, I guess the joke (if there is one) is on her. This one is both, Di, - my very last diary and my last will and testament. I'll try this one her way, anyway - just let my thoughts flow - keep the language simple - keep the words small - just make it sound like a regular guy after school at the soda shop.

I've decided that I want to live to be seventeen, and that happens officially, tomorrow night at 11:35 p.m. It's now 11:45 a.m. on the 4th of July 1952. That gives me 36 hours to live. There is a lot I want to get done. There are people I want to visit one last time; notes I need to write to certain precious folks; places I want to see one last time; things I want to do one last time; thoughts I want to think, and questions I want to ponder just one final time.

The first thing I want to do - stop - did you hear that, Di? I said, "Things I *want* to do." It seems like I haven't just done what I *wanted* to do for years. It's been, "Do what Mom and Pop want. Do what the school wants. Do what Mr. Elzer wants. Do what the other kids want. Do what's right. Do what Parson says I must. Do this for so and so, that for so and so, and on and on and on..." Well, Di, during these next (last) 36 hours, I'm just doing what I want to do!! I can't believe how GREAT that feels! (double smiles)

Back to the schedule. I'm going to take the first hour (beginning in about ten minutes) and write about my life - the way I have experienced it. None of that will be new to you, Di, but I'll bet it would knock the socks off most the folks in this little town who think they know me! Then, sometime during each hour, I'll write about what I have done during that hour - how I have felt, anything that seems important. I'll split some of the hours between doing and writing. Other hours, I'll just sit and write about things that are important to me. (I have quite a list here of those sorts of things.) In all honesty, I've written a couple of things out ahead of time because I was afraid, I wouldn't have time to do it all in these last few hours. I'll just insert those longer, prepared things into the diary where they belong.

I believe this is the best way to explain why this has happened, how it came to be, how my mind has been working (or not working, perhaps!). For some reason, Di, I really do want them all to know these things, and yet I haven't been able to come right out and tell anybody. I suppose I feel as though they wouldn't listen anyway - at least they wouldn't hear what I mean. Like last week, when Mr. Elzer bawled me out for forgetting to cover the pickle barrel before I left the store for the night. I responded by saying, "What do you want me to do, kill myself?" He chuckled and said, "That'll be the day!" Then he ruffled up my hair and apologized for yelling at me. (Boy, I hate it when people ruffle up my hair!) (triple frown)

But back to the point - who'd listen, anyway? Mom would, but she's the last one I'd ever want to bother with these kinds of thoughts. Doc would and Parson, maybe, but same for them - I don't want to upset them. Nobody else around here would take that kind of talk seriously from good old, well adjusted, smiling Craig Franklin. (plastered on, well-practiced, cover-up smile)

12:00 Noon, July 4, 1952
36 hours to live

Dear Diary,

I really have loved Mom and Pop Franklin. They took me in when my own family died in that Christmas Eve house fire and cared for me all by themselves these past fifteen years. They didn't have to do that. They were way too old to take on a two-year-old and then, later, much too old to handle a teenager. They are good people. The kind I would strive to be if I were to grow up. I'm really glad Pop is no longer here, so he won't have to go through this terrible hurt. Poor Mom - so old and so alone.

All that aside, however, it's been really tough to be an orphan - not knowing your own parents - not knowing what you came from. Of course, I've gleaned bits and pieces - my real Mother and Father were quite intelligent - Father, with an engineering degree and Mother a professor out at the college. Remember, Di, that conversation I had with Doc when I was thirteen - well, I guess it was that conversation *he* had with me. There in his office, I got the adult version of the birds and bees talk we had also had years earlier. Remember how that day he hinted that my Father had most likely been an alcoholic, and that's why he came here and was working as a clerk in a store instead of using his education. And how Doc said that, although it hadn't been proved for sure yet, he believed that the tendency toward being a drunk probably was inherited - how, therefore, he advised me to never, ever, even take that first sip of alcohol. I haven't, you know, Di. I've never taken that first sip, and I don't plan to. (Today, Di, that somehow seems humorous - couldn't hurt me much, now, could it!) (smile)

I always wished Father had been able to have that facts of life talk with me. I wonder what he'd have said. I guess I feel cheated on that count.

Well, back to my story. There are all kinds of other nice people in this little town who helped take care of me. You know, Di, by the time I was five, I'm sure I had milk and cookies – if not breakfast – in every kitchen in town, and that my face had been scrubbed spic and span in every bathroom. (smile) I still don't really know if these people treat me nice because they like me for 'Craig, the person,' or just because they feel sorry for 'Craig, the orphan.' My how I wish I knew! (frown - tear)

I was always safe here. Everyone watched out for me. I'm grateful for that - really, I am - but ... Well, you know how, when, as a kid, you leave somebody's house or store, and they usually say something like, "So long. Behave yourself, now." Well, to me they always said, "So long. Be good to your parents, now" (or words to that effect - that's what I always heard, anyway).

Kids with their real parents could misbehave or get into trouble, and it was okay, because real parents were expected to put up with those things, but me, I didn't dare do any of those normal things. I always had to be appreciative of Mom and Pop's generosity and - what's the word - altruism. Sometimes, Di, I hated them for being such good-hearted people and for not being my real parents. If Pop had just once really beat me like Harley's Dad beat him, then, perhaps, I could have felt free to be like a real kid - to get angry at them and things like that. No such luck! I'd just have to go on being perfect little 'Craigy.'

That's another bone I've had to pick with them over the years (but, of course, never did). When they took me in, they gave me a different name (Craig) from the one my natural Mother and Father wanted me to have. I've gone through most of my life by the wrong name! Now, I'm sure I am really not the person that I would have been, had Mother and Father raised me. I would have probably thought differently about many things, looked at people differently - just been a very different person from the one I have learned to be in Mom and Pop Franklin's home. I suppose I really am more a 'Craig' then, aren't I? If there is a next life, I wonder which name I'll go by there?

I've been so lucky to have one very best friend ever since I can remember being alive - Dear, dear Ginny. (warm, warm, smile) She and I have had very few secrets from one another - until now. It wouldn't be fair to tell her about my decision, now. She'd feel guilty for not being able to talk me out of it. Or, maybe, I'm afraid she would. At any rate (I say that a lot, don't I ?), she won't know. I'll write her a note later on - I have it on my schedule.

I've always been smart - I mean, I could always learn new things a whole lot quicker than anyone else my age and I don't forget. They all thought that must be so great. It is, I guess, in some ways, but it has also been one of the most terrible things in my life. Our school is a small one. Each room had double classes - first and second grades in one, third and fourth in another, and so on. In first (which I started at five), I learned all the second-grade work too, so they skipped me right on to third. In third, I learned the fourth-grade work, so, of course, they skipped me right on to fifth, and so on, year after terrible year. I started High School at nine - can you believe that! How dumb can adults be! (frown) How did they ever expect me to fit in with the kids there? It didn't matter how far ahead I skipped; I still learned all the material far faster than any of my classmates. As a result, I ended up having nothing in common with my fellow students academically and certainly nothing in common with them as people. It was so very scary always being around those great big kids! Most days I'd have given anything to be just average.

Remember my reaction to that first high school gym class? A scrawny little, 58-pound, lily-skinned, sandy headed, nine-year-old body, showering with all those great big, hairy, smelly guys. They teased and shoved me around a lot.

I know, now, that they were just horsing around like we teenagers often do. They were having fun for themselves, without so much as a thought about my feelings. I suppose it is behaviors such as that, that lead adults to call us 'mindless adolescents.'

I always took a lot of teasing - being an 'egg-head', 'a shrimp', 'an orphan', and on and on and on! And, I always just smiled and laughed with them and took it, even though, each time, those words hurt me so deeply I wanted to run away screaming and crying. Just because I could take it, didn't mean I liked to take it. (quadruple frown, and buckets of tears)

Remember, Di, the brilliantly fiendish plans I'd concoct here in your pages - ways to take glorious revenge on each and every one of them! (Smile with raised eyebrows) I could probably publish those as, *A Primer of Tantalizing Tortures*. I'm glad I never did those same kinds of hurtful things to others. I guess, in a way, then, all that pain served some purpose, didn't it? There must have been some easier way to learn that lesson, though, don't you think, Di?

Finally, after two miserable years in high school, I began college - a full scholarship at eleven! The scholarships, over the years, have been godsends. I would have never gotten there any other way. Having this little college right here in Springfield was another fortunate happenstance.

So, now, here I sit at sixteen, with a bachelors' degree in pre-med and education, and a master's degree in psychology, and no one willing to employ me. I understand that, but what's the 'boy genius' supposed to do now? - just stay in college until I finally grow up and people start taking me seriously - Gee, by that time I'll have *five* degrees!

You know, Di, it's taken me all this time, but I've finally realized that the answers to life's really important questions aren't found in books or classes or degrees. They're found by living, by trying out all sorts of different things, by getting to know all kinds of people - by listening and watching and reading between the lines. When, in my case, my school opted for books, rather than for peers, they pretty well spoiled that, didn't they! Now, I'm just too tired, too confused, too far behind to embark on that search.

I got off the track here somewhere, Di. (I know, no surprise to you!) I skipped over most of my early life. I wonder why - those were my very best years - up 'til about eight, maybe nine, I'd say. We lived just outside of town, and when I say 'just' I mean it. The sign saying Springfield, Pop. 1,006, was in our side yard. Our house is a white, three room places with a full attic, half of which I converted into my bedroom. It has been a great place to live and grow up. I've had a huge lawn to play in; tall trees to climb; a hill sloping down in back to the creek; a small orchard with fresh apples and pears (and cherries, when we could beat the black birds to them!); a board fence to walk like a tight rope; and, all of this, only five blocks from the stores down town. Truly, the best of all worlds for an active, energetic, little social-being like I was, when young.

We were really poor, with Pop being sick, and only Mom supporting us by taking in washings and ironings. Pop felt so guilty, I know, and Mom worked so hard - so many hours each day, six days a week (never on Sunday). She never ever complained, as far as I know. She used to tell me that the ability to work hard was one of God's greatest gifts. I remember one hot summer day when still a very little boy - watching Mom ironing there in the blistering heat of our kitchen. - I noticed the sweat from her forehead dropping down onto the shirt she was ironing, and I commented that she didn't even need to dampen the clothes today - her perspiration was doing that for her.

I'll never forget that half-smile that broke across her face - not much of a smile - just enough to know it was there - one of those where the chin and bottom lip are drawn up a bit and the edges of the mouth just barely turn up. It was such a tired smile coming from such a worn-out face. I suppose that was the first time it struck me how old they were - Mom and Pop - how tired they were, how really poor we were. I was frightened. What would become of me if something happened to them?

Mom always said that being poor had its wonderful side and that being rich had its sad side. Since I was poor, I got to plan and create the things I wanted - a wagon, a trike, a bike, a bunk bed. I got to enjoy all that time spent in the creative process - something that the poor rich kids never got to know and feel and appreciate. They just went out and bought stuff! I always, even to this day, have felt sorry for others who had to depend on 'store-bought' goods. They really do miss out on the most fascinating and rewarding part of life - creating! I'm sure that's one major reason I have usually been such a good problem solver. I've had a lot of practice!

Everyone has always asked me to solve their problems for them. There were Mrs. Steven's sick house plants; Old Mr. Black's squeaky floor; the school flag pole, when the pulley on top broke; the perennial leak in the church roof; the girl-friend/boy-friend problems of every kid in town, the parent's problems with their kids; even Parson, when he couldn't get through to Harley.

I guess I enjoyed that role, but it's been as terrible burden. When I'd ask people about my own problems or questions, they'd typically pat me on the head (boy, I hate that!) and say, "I'm sure you, of all people, will be able to solve that one for yourself." (disgusted frown) Ginny was really the only one who always listened - always tried to help - always cried with me when I hurt, laughed with me over the foolish things, and was proud with me at my accomplishments. If, in death, you miss those you have left behind, I will truly miss my Dear Ginny.

One thing nobody (except, I guess, Ginny and Mom) ever understood about me was that, except for being super-smart, I was really just a kid. I wanted other kids to like me. I wanted to be good at sports. I wanted good looking girls to chase me (and, of course, to catch me!). I wanted to be a good dancer, to look good, to always say just the right things. I didn't want the other kids to think I was a 'goody-goody' - probably failed there, completely. (sad frown) I didn't want my parents running my life. I wanted to try daring new things, to be invited to parties - the very best parties. I wanted friends who just took me as I was - who were neither intimidated by, nor overly impressed by, my 'smarts.'

Di, do you realize that last paragraph was all written in the past tense - like life is already over. Well, I guess essentially it is. In these last few hours I've begun to feel detached, distant - sort of like I'm looking down on Springfield and all its people from up above or from 'outside,' somehow. It's hard to describe.

Well, this first, of the last 36 hours, is about over. How do I summarize seventeen years? I am glad I had the opportunity to live with love - to learn the trials and rewards of hard work - to learn how to turn being poor into a creative, wonder-filled experience. I was fortunate to have been able to learn so very much, so very easily - though had it been more difficult, I might appreciate other people's struggles more.

I'm truly sorry that I've been such a burden on Mom and Pop and the good people of Springfield. I didn't mean to be. I'm sorry I couldn't find some way to make (help?) people just like me for the me that I am. I regret not being able to be a better person - though I guess I truly regret even more, the lofty standards these townspeople seemed to set for me (but no one else). How could such a thing have happened? And, worse yet, I suppose, why was I gullible enough to think I had to accept those standards as my own?

I'm sorry I turned out to be such a freak - orphan, genius, poor - you know. I'm sorry I won't have time to repay all the debts I've racked up - not money debts so much as the debts of caring and support, of love and opportunities. I know I should stick around and care for Mom - that's what I feel the worst about, but for once in my life, I am going to be selfish and take care of me first! My world has set impossible goals everybody expects me to achieve. The best and worst trait I have, I suppose, is to never allow myself to let anybody down. Best in that I have truly been helpful. Worst in that there is no way I can continue living up to such a standard.

I guess that's it, Di. Seventeen years of life "in three thousand words or less," as the contest rules on cereal boxes always said.

Well, now I have a few folks I need to visit one last time. Later, I'll tell you about each one, Di.

1:00 PM, July 4, 1952
35 hours to go

Dear Diary,

I stopped by old Mrs. Steven's place. She was in her rocker on the back porch - like usual. She had a big sugar cookie for me - like usual. I weeded her flower patch by the steps as we chatted - like usual. We talked for fifteen minutes or so about nothing of any real importance (who did what, how hot it was, the price of eggs went up again, Mr. Kopek at the park got a new flag for the 4th, Julie White hurt her ankle and probably won't be able to march with the band in the parade later on today). It was a great conversation because it really said, "We care a whole lot about one another - just being together is sufficient - nice - the words we say aren't really important at all."

I suggested to her that John needed some work to help pay for summer camp, so she might ask him to mow her lawn instead of me - I wasn't going to be able to continue.

That sure was a good cookie! I still remember the first one I ever had. I was about three, I guess. It was so good that I "took" an extra one and stuffed it inside my shirt when she wasn't looking. Mom found it when I got home and marched me right back to apologize. Up to that point in my life, that apology was the most fearsome big deal I'd had to endure. Today, I thanked Mrs. S. for playing the scene just right that day - It became an indelible lesson in honesty that has never left me. She will miss me

Then we talked about being young and being old. Mr. S. has been alone since she was thirty - that's when her husband was killed - forty years ago. I asked her why she didn't remarry. She said it just wasn't the thing to do back then - a widow remained a widow - true to her husband's memory. She seemed proud she had done it that way. Seemed senseless to me to be alone for forty years, but then it's her life.

I asked her about being lonely. She said not to confuse being "alone" with being "lonely." "I am alone, but never lonely. I have my wonderful memories of my life with Walter, and then, every few years, I get a whole new generation of young companions - like you, Craig - to bake cookies for."

She's right. Every kid in town has weeded her flowers with her and talked over every conceivable problem a young life can meet (save one, perhaps). Let's see, at probably six to ten cookies a day, 365 days a year for forty years - that must be over 100,000 cookies she's given away - 100,000 little pieces of happiness - well, pleasure, at least. So, over my fifteen years, I've probably eaten close to 5,000 all by myself - at, say three ounces each - that's several tons of Mrs. Steven's sugar cookies. No wonder I am so sweet!! (A bad joke, Craig. I mean really, really bad!!)

One at a time they didn't seem like so much, but... I guess that's the way with most really nice, enduring relationships - it's never a whole lot all at once that makes them so special. It's the accumulation of all the nice little things along the way that end up counting the most.

About that "lonely" thing. My life has been just the opposite of hers, I guess. I've never been "alone", really, but still, I've always felt very "lonely".

Mrs. Stevens doesn't like growing old. I think it's scary for her. She can still pretty well take care of herself, but what happens when she can't? She doesn't want to be a burden on anyone. But on whom will she be a burden? She has no family - no relatives still alive. (That's one thing she and I always shared - it made me feel close to her, somehow.)

I wonder what will happen to her. It's a shame for someone who has given so much to the kids in this town for so long, to have to worry so much about just getting old. It's not fair at all. You live a good life, help take care of all the kids in town, grow old and then have to be terrified about what will happen to you. No thanks - not for me! I'll take my leave early. (A coward? Yes, probably!)

I guess the scary parts of living never stop. It's so scary to be a little kid when everyone around you is bigger and rougher and faster and more skilled at just about everything! Then, it's scary in school - the tests, the homework, the bullies, the competition, and even the principal. Teen years are the worst that way, I guess - who really likes you and why, how you look to others (and what to do about it), being liked by the opposite sex, understanding and controlling and finding "proper" outlets for all these teen years feelings. Planning your future. Working out things with your parents - disagreements, money, hours, friends, jobs. Eventually, having to leave that home, and to face the big world on your own.

I used to think that once I got past sixteen, life would begin to level out and be really good. I'd be one of the 'big guys' by then (but, it seems, there are always bigger guys). I thought that surely by then I'd have this sexual thing all worked out, but, that just keeps getting stronger and more difficult to understand. I thought I'd make peace with my parents and work out an adult-to-adult relationship with them. (Face it, I'll always just be Mom's little boy - oh, she could respect me and my achievements and that's great, but she'd always treat me like her dear little Craigy, not as a grown up. Maybe that's normal?)

I thought that I would be able to finally just live to please myself and not have to worry about others anymore (just more and more people to be responsible for, and later on, a wife and children and someday Mom and maybe even Mrs. Stevens - just too much!).

I'd hate to get old - having young folks just think I was in the way, slow, sick, and unimportant. I know I hardly ever think about old people as if they had once been my age - young and vigorous - or that someday I'd be old and slow like them. I seldom really stop to think how the old people I see around town probably spent most of their life doing a fine job of taking care of others and being really nice people. I just get impatient with them - like when they take too long finding the change in their purse at the Post Office stamp window, or when they drive their cars so-o-o-o slowly and I'm in a hurry (but then, I'm always in a hurry - I'm sixteen!). I forget that one day most of us youngsters will end up just that same way. If I were to grow old and slow down and get confused sometimes, I'd sure hope the young people around me would be patient and understanding and even helpful.

I'd hate to slow down and know I was bothering others - younger people, in particular. I'll bet most of the old people feel that way too, don't they? When they hear one of us yell, "Hurry up, Pops," they are probably saying to themselves, "I know I'm a bother to you, young man. I wish I weren't - I'm sorry for having gotten so old. Believe you me, Sonny, I hate old age even worse than you do!"

Enough of that bleak gloom and doom! I ran into Officer Breck in front of the police station. You know, Di, how I've told you about the way he always squeezes the guy's shoulders while he talks with us. How I always hated that because I thought it hurt so. I realized today that as I was growing up, that squeeze was never really harsher than I could stand at the time. Pretty light when five. Some harder by ten. Quite man-to-man now. I think it is his way of saying, "I like you well enough to touch you, but I want you to understand that I am in charge around here, and if you ever need it, I will control you." At least that's the message that got through to me.

Actually, thinking back now, it was nice to know he was around. I behaved better knowing he was there - just that little nudge I needed sometimes to keep me on the straight and narrow. He worked my shoulder over, but good, today, Di, but you know what, today that hurt felt like love...

Well, Di, I have to move along - there are lots of my possessions that I want to get to certain people. I'll be back shortly to tell you how it went.

2:00 PM, July 4, 1952
34 hours to go

Dear Diary,

Di, do you remember my writing about Jerry Winston - he's living with Joe and Martha Reynolds over the hardware store — he's their nephew, I think - well, I found out his birthday is on the 6th, so I just took him my collection of Spike Jones records. He's always after me to come over to my place and listen to them. Boy, was he surprised! I know life's tough for him right now - I hope the records will help make things seem at least a little better. Told him I just couldn't take them with me to the university in September.

I'll miss being able to give things to people. It really tickles me deep down inside to see other people so happy because of me. That's a great power, you know, Di - to be able to make other people happy. It seems most everyone can make others sad without even trying but making them happy - that's a real art - it takes a lot of practice to be able to figure out just what somebody else needs at a certain time. I think I have been very good at that. I know that sometimes I did it just so someone would like me better. That probably was wrong - but it still did make them feel good, so it couldn't have been all bad, could it?

Mostly, I did it, I think, because I knew what it did for me when someone else was nice - even a stranger just saying, "Hi, how ya doin' ", made me feel so good, and safe, too, I guess. Just to know those strangers out there were really friendly people, too, and that I didn't have to be afraid of them. I always spoke to everybody I met, whether I knew them or not. (Got that from Pop.) For just that reason, I guess, to let them know other people - like me - were friendly and kind and safe to be around.

Maybe if everyone were that way, we wouldn't have all the wars and killing and unhappiness and suspiciousness that seems to have swept the World.

I guess I also give things to people and do things for them to help pay back all of the things everybody's done for me. Nobody in this town ever really had to do anything for me. I wasn't theirs. I wasn't even born here. They really didn't even know my parents all that well - we'd been in town less than two years when the fire happened. But, none of that seemed to matter. These people just took me in - It's like the whole town raised me. They were in most ways nice people who, I know, meant well.

They didn't realize how all of their differing advice confused me and tore me apart. Should I look out mostly for myself, like the barber would tell me, or should I put others first, like Parson and Mrs. Stevens would say? Should I stay here in Springfield and spend my life repaying my debt to the town, like Mr. Ames said, or should I get out and move on to bigger and better things I could only accomplish elsewhere - like Chicago or Indianapolis or St Louis - the way my teachers advised? How do you ever know what's really right?

If I'd just had Mother and Father's advice to go on, I don't think I'd be so confused about everything. Don't get me wrong - Mom and Pop gave great advise - I just never knew if it was the same that Mother and Father would have given. Who knows, maybe my real parents would have given me lousy advice. No, I'm going to believe it would have been great! I wonder, though, if, coming from them, I'd have listened to it at all - Billy and John sure don't take any of their parents' advice! (smile) No, I'm going to believe I would have listened to it.

Now that I am thinking about it, Di, I really don't think there is a *me*. It's me the way I am when I'm with Mom or Mrs. Stevens. The me I am when with Billy and John. The me at school. The me at Church. The me when I'm working at the grocery store. The me on a date. Those are really all very different me's! Which one, is really me? I guess the closest thing to the real me is when I'm with Ginny. We grew up together. I don't ever remember not having Ginny to play with or talk with or depend on. We never – well, seldom – had any secrets from one another. Boy, could we blackmail each other if we ever wanted to! And, some of the stuff we've done together! It's a wonder we're still alive! Skinny dipping at the creek back before we were even school-age - Exploring Wilson's Cave as eight-year olds - Jumping the gorge on bikes last summer.

I remember when we were about eight. I wanted to play

doctor like we had often done before, but Ginny said, "No, Mama says big girls don't play doctor with boys. Big girls just kiss them." So, I kissed her. What a disappointment! Playing doctor was much better! I suddenly knew for sure and certain that big girls were just not going to be any fun at all! (smile of all smiles!)

Although I've never kissed Ginny again, I guess I have done my share of kissing after I once reached thirteen or so. So did Ginny - just never together. It's been so great having a girl for a best friend and not having to mess up the relationship with the usual boy-girl stuff. Next to Mom, I love Ginny most. I hope I've helped her as much as she's helped me. Probably not. She's one super person. I'm sorry to be leaving her. She'll understand eventually, but she'll be sad and lonely for a time, just the same.

She'll probably be the only one who *will* understand! She knows how empty I feel. How I feel like there is not a real me inside. How so much of what I want to do and accomplish and have, are all so far out of reach. How scared I am to try any more. If I failed, I would be letting so many folks down. It turns my stomach just contemplating it.

We talked last night about how, if I left Springfield, and took the university scholarship to work on a Ph.D., I'd probably end up being rich and maybe even famous - two things that really scare me! I've seldom had more than ten dollars in my pocket at once - not for me to spend on me, at least. I wouldn't know what to do if I had unlimited resources. It doesn't seem like it would be any fun that way. I'd never get to plan ahead and save for something special. I'd probably not have time to make my own stuff anymore.

It's bad enough now, not knowing why people like me. If I were to become the rich Dr. Franklin, I'd certainly never know, would I? Ginny, of course, pointed out that I wouldn't have to live like I were rich, and that I could give a lot of my money away - maybe even take care of other orphans or fund research to cure polio and cancer and diabetes. She's probably right - Ginny usually is - but still, it's just way too scary. Way too much responsibility. That's what I'd call my autobiography, 'Way too much responsibility'.

My brief and limited experience with fame - High School

graduate at eleven, College graduate at thirteen, a graduate degree at fifteen - it's been terrible. You have no privacy. Every "doctor" in the country thinks he has the right to talk to me and to test me and to 'pick my brain.' Fame really stinks! (a page of frowns) I'm going to stop thinking about those things now.

Life is so confusing. Why must it be that way? I can master any textbook in a week, but I can't even come up with one convincing reason why to go on living. I can swim faster than any other sixteen-year-old in the State. I made first chair, first seat, First-band at the High School All-State Band Festival when I was eleven. I won the Literary Guild's writing award that same year, and the State Art Association's Best of Show medal in sculpture. My science fair entry won national honors.

Seems like I've had a lot of success, doesn't it, Di! But I've always been expected to be the best - Mom and Pop and teachers and friends. If I'd ever just placed second, I'd have let them all down. I could have cared less. I'd have given anything to just swim for the heck of it. To sculpt or play my clarinet, just for fun. To just tinker in the science lab because I wanted to play around with some idea. But I was expected to excel in everything I tried.

If I joined a club, I was elected president. If I took a job, I was made foreman. I never just got to be one of the kids. I even had to dress better - not more expensively - I'd never have been able to do that - but my shirt had to be pressed - my pants had to be spotless - my shoes had to be shined. Billy and John didn't have to be that way. Ginny didn't either. Nobody else (besides Mayor Betts, I guess) had to be so impeccable.

I'd walk in from recess: "Your shirt tail is out, Craig." I'd go into the cafe after school: "You have some dirt on the seat of your pants, Craig." I'd go to Church: "Your tie isn't pulled up tight, Craig." How did all this develop? Why? Who made up all those rules just for me? Why couldn't I change them? Why wouldn't the people in my life just leave me alone so I could find out who I really was deep down inside, and figure out what *I* wanted to do with my life?

Well, I guess I'll have the last laugh after all, won't I, Di! I will do with my life all that seems left to do with it. The only thing I have strength enough to do with it. That one thing that will free me - all of the me's - from everyone else's expectations - that will finally bring me peace.

It's already happening, you know, Di. Ever since I made the decision. I feel free! I know I said it before, but it is such a wonderful, carefree feeling. Carefree! As often as I've used that word, I never really understood what it meant until just now. I can't ever remember feeling like this before. Just me - doing just what I want to do. It's a lot like those moments in which I'm falling off to sleep at night. I know that in just moments I will be able to put all my cares and fears and problems away for a while and just slip off into a slumber of peace and freedom. I think that's just exactly what my last moments of life will feel like. I can hardly wait!

First, though, I have a few more things to give away. My blue sport coat goes to Jimmy Wills - I know it's too big now, but he'll grow into it. His folks will never be able to afford one for his prom. I want Austin to have my library. He appreciates knowledge the way I have. He is so smart! I do hope not too smart. I told him to expect them. He thinks he's going to take care of them for me while I'm off at the university.

My files, filled with things I've written, must go to Mrs. Heatherton at the High School (after Mom and Ginny take out what they want, of course). Mrs. Heatherton is the one who most encouraged me to write. Perhaps as she reads through my stuff, she'll figure out that schools may really be able to help other smart kids more, by just not trying so hard to help them. I'll leave a note to make sure she gets them.

My clarinet will go to the band director, Mr. Childs. He'll make sure some new student gets it - someone who will appreciate it and take good care of it - someone, I hope, who can just play it for fun! My ball glove is for little Perry. I want him to have something that he knows has been extra special to me. He has such a rough, rough road ahead.

Well, it looks as though I have a lot of deliveries to make. This may take some time.

3:00 PM, July 4, 1952
33 hours to go

Dear Diary,

Well, Di, most everything is now either delivered or I've made arrangements for them to get to where they belong. I used up almost all my writing time this hour running around. That's okay, I need to get a head start on next hour's entry anyway. I want to examine all my fears. That may take days, huh, Di! (smile, frown)

4:00 PM, July 4, 1952
32 hours to go

Dear Diary

You're so lucky, Di. You can't be afraid of things. Pop used to say that being afraid of some things was smart - some things should be frightening, like, for a three-year-old, being out in the street should be frightening - that keeps him on the sidewalk where he can be safe. Having a loaded gun held against your head should be frightening, otherwise folks would regularly be blowing holes in their heads. Nazis and fascists and dictators and race-haters should be frightening, because they can destroy man's freedom - his basic dignity - his right to live life freely as he deems right and proper.

Those aren't the kinds of fears I'm concerned about right now, Di. I'm thinking back about all the things I've been afraid of over the years - so many things - Monsters under my bed at night. (At five, I felt so smug when I began sleeping on a mattress on the floor – take that, monsters!) You know, still at sixteen, I sometimes get that same prickly chill up my spine and feel a rush of adrenaline when I'm out walking alone real late at night. I mean, I know it's not a monster, but what might it be? I sometimes think it was easier back when I new exactly what to be afraid of - monsters - than now, when I'm not so sure what's out there. At least, when small, I knew I'd recognize a monster when I saw one. Now, I'm not really sure how my "monsters" may appear.

I got really scared when they began skipping me ahead in school - I'd have to leave my old friends - be with older guys with whom I knew I couldn't compete in games and sports. By seventh grade, when I was eight, the other guy's normal play was just terribly rough and very hard on my immature little body. Recess became such a frightening time. Most of them weren't trying to hurt me - I knew that even then - it just happened. Twice a day, every day, all school year long, I had to be terrified and, of course, never, ever let on - wouldn't have been 'manly.'

I used to be afraid - I guess that's the right word - of making my parents angry. I had never really seen them angry - at me or anything else. I had seen Harley's Dad knock him across his bedroom. I didn't want Mom or Pop to ever have to get angry like that with me. More than angry, I guess, I didn't want Mom and Pop to have to be disappointed in me - with me. I wanted, so much, for them to be able to be proud of me. I felt like @#$%&* when I thought they were not proud of me, let alone when they might be outright disappointed in me.

The first time I can remember that I disappointed Mom was when I "stole" that sugar cookie from Mrs. Stevens. I guess it was the first time I began to realize how I had the power to really hurt someone else in a non-physical way, and in that instance, to unintentionally hurt two people I would never want to hurt. From then on, I had to be on guard - a huge responsibility for a three-year-old, wouldn't you say, Di?

I've always been afraid of not fitting in with the other kids and not being accepted by them. (Wonder why!) (frown) Somehow, I was always pretty much able to get them to accept me - even the bigger kids - as I progressed through school. I was different enough, I guess, that I wasn't a real threat to most of them. Who ever felt the need to compete with a twerpy little genius! So, they accepted me for what I was on that count, but still, I never really felt that I fit in socially - not with my classmates, anyway. I seemed to believe I should have when I really shouldn't have.

Once school was over for the day, I'd high tail it for the park and the kids my own age. There, I fit in better. When I got to High School, the difference was really magnified. When all the other freshman boys were talking dirty about girls and sex, I really had no idea what was going on, and I most certainly could not believably fit into any of those conversations. But

26

then, after school, back in my own neighborhood, I could play catch, build in the sand box, swing to my heart's content, wrestle with the other guys my age, and dig holes to China with Billy and John (Knowing that was impossibility never curbed my enthusiasm.)

Mostly, I felt I fit in, there. The younger kids (my age, I mean) didn't all accept me, either. It was hard to convince other nine-year-olds that you were just one of the guys when you'd let words slip out like, morose, when you meant sad, indisposed when you meant sick, and apprehensive when you meant scared! "Humpty Dumpty's back," (meaning "egghead") they'd taunt - well, a few of them would, anyway. I sure hated that! It was so hard remembering to use one set of vocabulary at school, another at home, and still another with my age mates and the townspeople.

When I was fourteen and really beginning to be genuinely interested in girls and all their wonderful "features," I was surrounded by college girls (women, really) who wouldn't take my amorous advances seriously. (Even *they* would sometimes pat me on the head - me, a fourteen-year-old!) It wasn't much better "back home," because all the kids who went to school together seemed to always be paired as couples before I got a chance to make my pitch.

So, you see, Di, no girls anywhere wanted me. I had to wonder if, perhaps, it wasn't just a jurisdictional problem, but that, in fact, I was just a twerp who girls would never like. (monumental frown) I once offered Sharon a hard-to-come-by dollar if she'd let me spend just ten minutes kissing her on the lips! I was so serious, and she took it as such a joke! (sigh, frown)

Well, eventually I did get started kissing the girls - and enjoying it just as much as I thought I would - and I got that all worked out, but, my, what a fearful time it had been.

It's funny about 'failing,' Di. I was thinking about it the other day - comparing Harley and me. Aside from his rotten disposition, he is really smart - not a genius - but he could make all A's and B's if he tried. For me, the fear of failing made me really apply myself - go all out - write twenty-page reports when only five pages were required, make ten book reports when three were required, and on and on and on. It spurred me on to just keep doing better and better - more and more. But Harley - I guess he has really never understood how smart he is. I think he was so afraid that he would fail in school (like his parents kept telling him he did around home!), that he never tried. It was like if he made it obvious to everyone that he wasn't trying, then no one would ever really know for sure how well he might have done if he had tried.

What a waste! Think of all the things he has missed because of that. But what do you do? I think he's really just as frightened inside as I have been, yet, like with me, most people don't ever see that side of him. In Harley, they only see the big, dumb, fearsome bully. In me, the 'million-dollar brain' wearing the big grin and having 'the World by its tail. (Just what is a kid supposed to do once he gets the World by its tail? What a scary concept! Draw it out as a cartoon in your mind, Di. A little kid with the whole big World by its tail. Downright terrifying!)

I think I only ever saw Pop cry twice. Once, just a few minutes before he died, when Mom leaned over and kissed him for the last time. He couldn't talk - he just looked up at her through his tired, tired eyes, as they filled up with tears. The other time was when I won the swimming marathon a few years ago. I ran out of the lake, up onto the beach, grabbed Mom for the first hug - then Pop! In the hubbub of the moment, I only got a brief glance, but there were tears on his cheeks. I rubbed my wet hair all over his face, as I grabbed him - to disguise his tears - seemed the necessary thing to do just then. I wonder why I had to protect him that way? Was I protecting his manhood, or my image of Pop? Maybe both. At any rate, he knew what I had done and as I released him from my long, long embrace, our eyes met ever so briefly. In that split second, I knew he was saying, "Thank you, Son," and he knew I was saying, "I know, Pop. It's Okay."

I guess I haven't cried in public since I was eight. We learn at a very young age here in Springfield that males don't cry. I missed the best parts of so many good movies because, on a date, I'd have to look away in order to not see the sadness on the screen and thereby avoid the risk of shedding some tears. DUMB! DUMB!! DUMB!!!

I cried enough back in my room at night to make up for it,

though. Boy, did I! Mom caught me crying in bed several times. She'd say, "Do you want to talk?" I'd lay my head in her lap as she sat on the edge of my bed. Sometimes we'd talk - Sometimes we'd just stay close. Mom made my world so safe, when I was small.

It didn't work so well once I got older. I wished it would have, but knew I had to fend for myself. So did she. No more tucking-in after my eleventh birthday. I'm not really sure why she chose that time to stop coming into my room at night.

Remember, Di, the hours I used to spend in front of the mirror. I still catch myself doing it sometimes. Back then, I so wanted my little boy's body to hurry up and mature so I could keep up with the older guys in my class at school. I'd search that mirror, day after day, for any sign that puberty might be approaching – upper lip, under my arms and other more obvious places.

And my face and hair - how I have agonized over my looks. Cute, as a little boy (when I could have cared less!). That faded to gawky by puberty, and then to very plain, indeed, these past several years. Oh, I wouldn't scare anybody off, but I've had to come to the realization that what I have, is all I'm ever getting - just plain and ordinary. I wonder how Mom feels about that. Interesting - I never wondered that wonder before.

I do wonder, how it came to be that handsome and beautiful often seem to be more important than nice and friendly. I've rated the kids in this town on looks. At the outside, only about ten percent of the boys would be considered really good looking and about the same for beautiful girls. That leaves the rest of us - 90% (a sizeable chunk of humanity) who aren't. Why, then, aren't the 'good looking' people the freaks and the rest of us the models? (furrowed brow) So strange! It seems unfair so many of us adolescents have to be so sad about the way we look, when, actually, we are what is normal!

So many things to be fearful of. People do grow into adulthood, somehow, though, don't they, Di. Maybe adolescence is 'God's' initiation for us into adulthood. (If that's true, God must be despicably sadistic!) (fiendish grin while rolling one's hands together) Giving Him the benefit of the doubt here for a moment, maybe adolescence is some kind of inoculation - a shot in the arm, so to speak - to prepare us for the 'slings and arrows' of adulthood. If we can endure and tolerate our teen years, we can then survive the problems of adulthood. I kind of like that last one. I almost wish I had the nerve to stick around and see if that's true.

It is so hard to be different - or at least to feel you are different - whether anyone else thinks you are or not. Especially when we are adolescents. I used to think I'd give anything to only have to deal with a teenage guy's normal three P's - Pimples, Parents, Parties. But even without all my freaky 'genius' and 'niceness' problems, the three P's would still be terrible enough, I guess. The thing that is sooo hard to keep in mind, is that in order to be an adult, all those people really did have to endure - live through - all this, and they did! (most quizzical expression) Well, not the genius parts.

You know, Di, it's amazing how little most adults seem to remember about being a teenager! They all give me the same line: "You are now enjoying the best years of your life!" If this is the best, I sure don't want to have to endure the rest. I'm not sure they really mean it the way it sounds, though. I think they must mean that the really good times - those times when I'm with my best friends, having a great time, acting absurd, and all my daily problems are pushed out of mind for a little while - that *those* times are those best times they mean. They are those momentary, carefree times before any of the true adult responsibilities or concerns or crises begin in earnest. That may be true, if you just focus on those good times, but surely, they can't also be including the adolescent's bad times as part of the best years of my life. Are they really saying that even my worst times right now are better than the worst times of adulthood? I must remember to bring up that one with Doc or Parson when I talk with them after while.

Di, you know how I enjoy reading Sigmund Freud, the psychoanalyst. It's like being on a fantasy-like safari through the deep, dark forests of a person's mind. Freud says we tend to forget experiences that are bad or unhappy and tend to remember only the good or better events. Perhaps that's what takes place in the adult mind - the agonizing side of adolescence fades, and the positive aspects remain. That could explain a lot - much as I hate to give old Siggy F. credit for anything other than entertaining reading. (smile through a goatee)

That process of 'forgetting' may be good for the individual - to forget the pain of adolescence - but I think it's extremely unfortunate for what it does to cross-generational understanding. The adults who seem to remember best how it really was, appear to me to be the easiest to relate to. They are often not the prettiest or most handsome, or most athletic or smartest people around. Maybe their high points as teens weren't so lofty as to over-shadow the 'normal' low points they experienced. Maybe that instills less repression, clearer perceptions, more realistic memories and more readily available empathy.

Well, Di, what am I saying? "That being a teenager has been scary enough for me – so being an adult must be simply terrifying!" (I hope I'm wrong.)

Another thing I've always been afraid of - making the wrong choices. How am I supposed to know, now, what the right choices are for later on? So often, it seems to be a choice between what I'm told is "right," and the alternative that appears to be so much more fun. I read some Puritan philosopher somewhere, and he said, "Work is the courtyard of God's temple, and pleasure is the Devil's playground." I'd rather believe the old adage that, "All work and no play, makes Johnny a dull boy!" (uncertain smile)

Why is it, that so much of what looks like fun, is held up by adults as being wrong? - close dancing, showing affection in public, new musical trends, just goofing off. I have noticed one thing about myself, Di. I can almost never take an adult's word for how something is probably going to turn out - I have to find out for myself. It's truly a wonder any of us live beyond fifteen! I man it really is. They've done things; they've learned good lessons; why don't we accept them and learn from their experiences? All the dumb and senseless stuff I have done just to see if . . . A lot of it outright stupidly dangerous, now that I am looking back on it!

I guess I always felt invincible - like nothing could harm me! I'm too smart to ignore the facts, so why won't I listen to advice? It certainly seems as though I don't trust adults to be telling me the truth. It's like I am saying, "If you tried it, don't tell me I can't try it!" - Yes, that's just the feeling I get! At the same time, I know how dumb that is, I also know that really is how I feel. Even from adults I know and trust on most things, like Mom and Pop and Doc and Parson - I always think they are somehow trying to pull the wool over my eyes when they try to give me advice about living my life right now.

That's a helluva mess, isn't it? I want to make my own choices even though it's so very scary that I really don't want to make my own choices. It is so very frightening to be frightened. Does that make any sense at all, Di? *Any* sense at all ?

I think that choices about the future are the worst. (Yes, I know, all choices are about the future - you can't choose about the past!) What I mean is, the more distant future, I guess. What shall I be? Where shall I live? Who shall I marry (and how will I know)? Who shall be my friends? Who, if anyone, shall be my enemies? How shall I handle my money? What beliefs should I pass on to my own children, and how can I really tell what is going to be right or wrong for them fifty years from now in this rapidly changing world?

See, Di, being a genius doesn't make life all that much easier. Here I sit, not knowing the answer to even one item on that list of questions. (and you should see the size of my *full* list!) Being smart means, I can see too many alternatives that regular folks just don't see. That makes choosing all the more difficult. I have so much more knowledge to sort through on the way to a decision. Nothing can be seen as just right or wrong. Everything is somewhere in between - shaded a bit more one way than another, perhaps, but never obviously black or white - right or wrong. It all gets blurred in a vast sea of gray.

Here's an example. One I've grappled with since I was very young. Most kids are told: "God created you and the universe and everything that's in it. God has always been and always will be. He can reward you or punish you for all eternity based on how well you live your life and how you worship Him." - Amen and Hallelujah! Now, most kids just accept that - it's too overwhelming a set of concepts to question, let alone analyze. Not old Craigy - oh no, boy, I was lying awake night after night questioning all those things way back before I was even seven years old.

That whole scenario just didn't make sense to me then, and it still doesn't today. Life would be so much easier if I could just go along with it - like most other people - but to say I do would be an outright lie – 'God', I'm told, punishes people who lie, so show me how to get out of this little bind, Di. Punished if I really don't believe or punished if I lie and say I do. I guess I'll just leave god for other people to use (or misuse). It's just not a concept I can fathom. I suppose those who can just accept it are the lucky ones.

Another tough choice, but one I've already had to make, isn't it? Well, if I'm correct, and all this god stuff is baloney, then when I die, I die, and that's that. It's all over. Period! (Sort of humorous, though. If, at death, it is really all over, I'll never know that I was right!) If I am wrong, then, I guess since I couldn't believe, no matter how good a life I have tried to live, I am still doomed to burn in hell. (Perhaps I'll ask to be buried with a fan, just in case!) (smile, shoulder shrug)

You know what I think scares me the most of all, Di? It's know-it-alls. People who are truly convinced that they really do know what is right and what is wrong - what should be and what should not be - how one should believe and how one should not believe - people who lay claim to knowing the truth and the only truth.

Now, those people are scary enough when they stay to themselves, but those kind never seem to do that. They feel that since they are the only enlightened people on Earth, it's their mission to make converts of everybody else. Well, I suppose I have to acknowledge their right to have their beliefs (a right, by the way, they don't allow me), at least so long as they don't hurt others. It certainly irks me to death (oops! Poor choice of words!) when they try to force that belief on others - on me, in particular, I suppose! Am I willing to hear their position? Of course, I welcome new ideas, but on *my* schedule, not theirs!

They scare me most, though, because, since they know they are right, they therefore so often feel free to use whatever means is necessary to convince and convert the rest of us. No room for discourse. No need for further information. It's open and shut. A closed mind is just terrifying to me!

Then, there are all those times I've felt I was forced to choose between my parents and my friends. To be a part of the group, I sometimes have had to do things I knew my parents couldn't approve. In fact, deep down inside, I didn't even really approve of them myself. Nevertheless, my choice was clear; do it, and be accepted by the other kids (the most important people in my life) but also be rejected by my parents if they find out, or don't do it, and risk alienation from my peers, when chances are high that my parents won't ever even find out that I did make the 'right' choice."

It's a lose-lose situation, sometimes, Di. It's walking a very, very tight rope if you let yourself be concerned about it (and, of course, I do! Have. Did?).

Most of the kids I know just seem to be able to turn off the concepts of 'right and wrong.' They just immediately replace them with the concepts of 'in or out,' 'accepted or rejected.' The usual inner consequence of doing 'wrong' is feeling guilty. The inner consequence of being 'out,' is, for teens like me, loneliness, at best, and despair or agony, at worst! I've decided that a 'normal' teenager never ever chooses loneliness, so I guess replacing the 'right and wrong' concept with the 'in or out' concept, is entirely normal, if not, inevitable. (Not necessarily right or safe or sensible, mind you, but normal.)

Just stop and think about that, Di. It is a terribly scary reality. Thousands upon thousands of us teenagers, regulating our every social act, based not on what's right and what's not right, but on what will get me in or keep me in, and protect me from being out!

I've been there, Di. I've been deep into it. Just the struggle associated with being in or out is all-consuming. When, as I have done, you also try to impose the right and wrong thing on top of it (only do 'right' things to get 'in', so not only will you not be lonely or left out, but so you will also not feel guilty), you tear yourself apart. I really doubt if you can use both sets of values simultaneously in most teen cultures. (I sound like Professor Bigalow!) Freedom to have our own beliefs is crucial, of course, in a free society like ours, but when those beliefs and goals and actions get too far removed from the basic values of that culture, it seems to me it takes a terrible

34

toll.

Let's see if I can say all that in Soda Shop words. When I have to stray too far from what I have been taught at home is right, just in order to be accepted by my friends, then I should pull back and reconsider the whole situation. (not bad, if I do say so myself! Would have been better with a chocolate shake!)

Add to this the fear I've always had that I might hurt someone - make them feel bad, or worst of all, feel worthless. I've always really tried to make others feel good - to be happy - to like themselves. That's abnormal, I guess, for a teenager. Many of the other kids, especially the girls, seem to always be running down who ever isn't around at the moment. To fit in, *you* seem to have to do it, too. Fitting in that way, just hasn't ever been more important to me than other people's feelings. I guess that's just one more, weird characteristic of good old Craig Franklin - boy freak!

Why do my friends have to spend so much time running other people down, Di? Parson says there are two ways of making yourself feel superior to others. One is to work hard and actually become superior (develop more skill, or more knowledge, or become more capable). The second way is to put other people down. Even though you don't really change yourself with this second method, you feel superior because you think you have made something less out of the other person. Belittling someone magically makes them less good than you??? Rubbish, of course!

That's really a 'sick' way to make yourself feel superior; don't you think? Perhaps it's an 'illness' that regularly infects most teenagers. In some people, it seems to be quite a temporary malady - they grow out of it as they enter adulthood. I'm not so certain about some of the others - look at Mr. Barns down at the feed store. He runs down everybody and everything - I feel so sorry for him.

My, this entry is getting long, isn't it, and, I'm afraid it doesn't sound much like that 'guy after school in the soda shop.' Maybe next hour.

Just one more comment, Di. I wonder why other kids don't react inside like I do when I know I've brightened someone else's day - made them feel a little better? Now, I don't mean they never do this and that they don't seem to get a momentary kick out of it. Many of them do. But I get an adrenaline rush that sets me up for the whole day! I feel so good all over. I know I'm probably happier than the person I helped. Do you suppose that the other kids get that same wonderful feeling when they have successfully made fun of someone or put them down or said crummy things about them? If they do, then I fully understand why they continue doing it. Next to an orgasm, it's the greatest feeling I have ever known - to make someone like himself a little better or to become just a little happier than before I passed his way.

If I were going to stick around this old, World a while longer, that's how I'd spend my life - I'd become the Johnny Appleseed of Smiles! (I believe I even tried that for a time when I was a little boy.) But, life in general is just too terrifying for me. It's hard to flash a smile any more that will pass as genuine. I'm just too terribly frightened deep down inside.

I have to wonder, Di, what my own son might think - say twenty-five years from now - if, as a sixteen-year-old, he'd find this diary and read it? Would things really be so different, then? Oh, sure, the fads will be different, the clothes will be different, the opportunities will be different, the technology will be greatly different, but I wonder if the kind of thoughts about fears, which I've set down here in hour number 32, will really be that much different, then?

Reading about how it was to grow up back in, even the most ancient of 'civilized' cultures, leads me to believe that even as the World changes and progress rushes on all around them, adolescence tends to remain a period in which time stands still - so to speak. The same kinds of concerns surface. The same problems must be faced. The same good times are available. The same reasons for despair, appear. The same mist dims one's clear view of the future. And still, most survive to become happy, productive adults.

Adolescence may just be the most enduring, the most unchanging, never-improving experience, the human species has ever produced. The one period in our life when, for some unexplained reason, we must totally ignore the lessons of history and go out and 'invent the wheel all over again.'

It seems as though most people are afraid of death -

strangely, even many of those who profess to believe in a life hereafter. Life comes. Life goes. I've never feared death. I certainly fear life more - at least right now. (I sure wish I hadn't thought those last four words. They open the possibility that in the future - if I were to allow myself a future - the fear of life might wane - diminish or leave altogether. I'll choose not to pursue those thoughts.)

I promise to be less stuffy next hour!

5:00 PM, July 4, 1952
31 hours to go

Dear Diary,

I just came from supper with Mom. She fixed my favorite meal for my birthday - ham, with green beans and yams and home baked brown bread. The Angel Food cake was complete with seventeen candles. I'm not sure that really is my favorite meal anymore, but Mom thinks so, and it's become a tradition. Regardless, it was great! It tasted exactly like birthday.

Mom has always been a great cook - even when we had hardly anything left in the house to eat, she'd whip up a Thursday Stew or a Celestial Casserole. (She always named strange dishes to make them seem more appealing, I guess.) They were always quite tasty to my way of thinking! Pop and I weren't much good in the kitchen and more than once had been told to skedaddle.

We got to remembering my past birthdays. She related that when I was three, and before anyone realized what was happening, I chewed up the candles and fashioned a, "horsey", from the wax. I seemed to enjoy the wrapping paper more than the gift. At four, I got new under shorts as my gift, so nothing would do but that I undress, right then and there, to try them on.

At five, since I was already reading everything in sight, Mom somehow obtained a used set of encyclopedias – The two-volume, Lincoln Library of essential knowledge. I still have them – something over 2,000 pages. It took me about two months to master those, she related. After that, she saw to it that I had access to wonderful books. She'd borrow them from the richer families for whom she washed. By ten, I suppose I had read just about every privately-owned book in Springfield. Mom said other mothers always complained about keeping their kids in clothes. Her problem was keeping me in books! (smile) Somehow, she always did!

Mom and Pop loved to read, too. Pop read more because, after he got sick, he had the time. Mom always had a book of some kind, open on the end of the ironing board, as she worked. "So many things to learn and do," she'd say, "And only one short lifetime in which to do it." I'm sure none of us contemplated then, just how short one lifetime might turn out to be.

Pop said, "Books are the road to freedom." He never explained that to me. Just said the older I became, the more I'd understand it. It didn't take me long to catch on. Freedom from ignorance - the more one knew the wider the opportunities one had. I learned to be interested in just about everything, just like Mom and Pop. My books were truly, gifts of freedom! (That would make a great book title, don't you think, Di.)

Mom also remembered about the year I wanted an American Flag for my birthday - a great big one to fly on the 4th of July. I was so sure I would get it, that, weeks ahead of time, I began building a flagpole out in front. Now, it had never entered my mind that Mom would buy a flag - she'd just sew one. So, when she gave it to me, I couldn't understand her apology for not having been able to afford a 'real' one from the store. I told her again today, how much better it was to have hers. Anyone could have one made on an assembly line, but mine was handmade - assembled with love - by my Mom! No one else will ever in all of eternity have one just like that. I still have it, Di. It's been flying out front on that same flagpole since dawn, this morning.

I told Mom that I wanted to be wrapped in it when I was buried. Her eyes welled up with tears and she put on her famous half-smile, patted my arm and changed the topic. To smile through pain and adversity was one of Mom's strengths that I always had admired. I wonder what her thoughts have been, there, behind those smiles. What has she really done inside of herself to endure all the hardships she's seen? Why couldn't I have learned just that one thing from her?

I looked at her face a lot during supper. She's seventy-three now, but she looks eighty-three. She looked so tired, and these past several months (perhaps just because I've been making such a point to notice things) she seems to be getting so thin. She says she's fine - but that's the only thing she's ever said.

I asked her, straight out, about her financial situation. Our money was something she and Pop never talked to me about. Surprisingly, she answered me tonight without so much as a blink. Says she has all she'll ever need. Pop's insurance from the Plant is still all in the bank and she's always put a little away each week.

I'm sure she has saved, though goodness knows I don't understand how, on as little as they ever had. Saving was important in our home - a left-over from the depression days, I guess. From the first dime I ever earned, I had to save ten percent for a 'rainy day,' give ten percent to people who needed it more than I did, and then, the rest I could use.

I still do that, long after it was required of me. I think it really does make life better to do it that way. I feel secure with a savings account to fall back on and I feel so good when I know that some of my money has helped somebody in need! That's really the best part! I've been thinking a lot about that these past few months. I think that one idea separates people into two distinct classes - those who are content to live a self-centered life and those who really see themselves as a part of the larger family of man - those who care and take care of one another - those who give their love freely. It makes me proud that I have been a member of the second group! (eternal smile)

Mom brought out some papers for me to sign. They put her bank accounts and the house in my name as well as hers. She said she'd just feel better getting these things taken care of now, before I left (for the university). I signed them, of course, because it obviously meant a lot to her. How could she know ... well.

It was so easy to talk with Mom at supper tonight. I mean,

we always talked okay, don't get me wrong, Di, but it was as if she wanted to remember things with me today, just as much as I wanted to remember with her. Probably because I haven't really made much time for her this past six months. At any rate, it was so comfortable - so nice - so warm - so family.

I got her remembering about Pop. Since he died last March, she hadn't talked much about him. Tonight, she even laughed out loud remembering some of the silly things Pop did while he was courting her. He was as dumb about girls at seventeen as I am! Who'd have ever thought that! (smile with furrowed brow) Perhaps some things really don't change so much from generation to generation!

She remembered the time when, unbeknownst to her, he had a big pimple on the end of his nose, the same day as the pie social at church. So, he provoked a fight with the town bully and got punched in the nose - all of this, so he could put a piece of tape on his nose to cover the pimple while making it seem as though he was just taping up an injury. An injury acquired in a fight was more acceptable than a pimple - even back in 1900! Not much has changed in these past 48 years, has it? I wonder how kids will be reacting to pimples 48 years from now? Maybe there will be a miracle medicine that will keep pimples from ever happening in the first place. Wouldn't that be great!

Speaking of pimples, I don't have any right now. I'm really happy about that because I'd hate for everyone to see me there in my coffin with a mess of pimples on my face – Gee Whizz, Di, how vain can a guy be!

"Gee Whizz," reminds me of back when I was trying out all the swear words - at about seven, I guess. As I'd be getting my mouth washed out with soap, I'd be protesting that the source was not really my tongue, but my brain, so it wasn't fair to attack my mouth. Mom would counter with, "I can't get to your brain, so I'll work on the opening that is closest too it!"

Bad words? I never really understood how some words - merely representations of real things - could be bad, and others, which represented exactly the same thing, were Okay. I could say, 'Gee Whizz,' but never 'Jesus.' I could say, 'Jimmy's mother wasn't married when he was born,' but I couldn't convey exactly the same message by saying, 'Jimmy is a bastard,' or 'Jimmy is a son of a bitch.'

Mom would say, "Small, crude, barren, uncreative minds use four letter words. You, Craig, can do much better than that!" She was right, I think. The habitual use of 'swear words' does seem to be the sign of an underdeveloped mind in a gigantic rut. Past the age of nine or ten, I chose not to swear (well, not very often, anyway). That was probably more because I didn't want to offend others, than that I, personally, found the words offensive. I must admit, it has become a wonderful game to find words and phrases which, in effect, do call someone a 'damn fool' or an 'S O B,' without that person ever realizing what I've said. I'm satisfied and delighted! They are confused! Mom, bless her good heart, is happy!

I was amused at Mom, tonight. She said there were three questions she had wanted to ask me for a long time but hadn't been able to bring herself to ask. Since we were sharing such a close and comfortable time, she decided to ask them. (Here comes that big, "Do you have sex with girls," question, I thought, but no!) (wipe sweat from brow while smiling sheepishly)

Her first question was, "Do you smoke?" She had smelled smoke on my clothing from time to time. Not knowing if it was from friends smoking or from mine, she had asked. "No, Mom, I don't smoke." (An easy one.) Then we remembered the time Pop caught me trying to smoke a cigar out back. We had a good laugh. Long ago I put that experience into a poem. I dug it out and read it to her.

My First and Last Cigar

At ten, it seemed I never would
Get grown up fast enough.
I'd try what grown-up things I could
To feel adult and tough.

A long cigar, I did procure.
Lit up behind our shed.
Now *this* was grown-up stuff for sure,
Just like the big boys said!

I inhaled long - took quite a puff -
Then gagged - thought I would die!
As I decided, "That's enough."
My Poppa happened by.

Red-handed caught, with no way out!
I'd had it now, I knew!
Some terrible punishment, no doubt,
Would very soon be due.

But he surprised me when he said,
"A smoker, now, I see."
"Not really, Pop. I'm done." I pled.
But THAT was not to be.

"I think," he said, "that you should smoke
This whole cigar, don't you?"
I thought, at first, it was a joke -
Not so - I soon turned blue!

Pop sat beside me there and talked
'Bout weather, work, and ball,
And then, when I was done, we walked
Back home - no guff at all.

Now folks, I had been sick before,
And I'd been filled with fear,
But never, ever, was I more
Afraid my death was near!

Until more grown, we never spoke
'Bout that cigar I had.
But ne'er again would this guy smoke -
All thanks to one wise Dad!

Her second question: "In all these years that you and your
boy friends have been skinny dipping in the creek under the
trestle, have you ever had girls there with you?" "Not by
design, Mom," I told her quite honestly. "Occasionally,

though, we knew some girls were peeking at us through the bushes, but we never had them actually join us - we never even let them know we knew they were there." (Now, between you and me, Di, I must admit we did 'strut our stuff' a bit more openly in their direction when we knew they were around, but that was just guy-ego stuff. It was always more a joke than anything else.)

Her third question was about drinking alcohol. I assured her I had never had a drop - I told her why. I could always have fun, always have a great time, usually even be the life of the party, in fact, without ever resorting to alcohol (or anything else, for that matter) for 'support' or 'courage'. I wanted to have fun naturally, not artificially and, the next morning, I wanted to remember the fun I'd had the night before. I always felt alcohol was only for those poor non-creative, unimaginative minds, too ignorant to figure out enjoyable alternatives to drunkenness - I feel very sorry for them.

I know some of the other guys were uncomfortable having me around when they were drinking. I'd see them making complete fools of themselves and, somehow, unless I also made a fool of myself, they were uncomfortable. I seldom went to their 'drink-fests' this past year because, after an hour or so, nobody talked sense (even though they thought they were utterly amusing and fantastically intellectual). I felt hurt and embarrassed watching my friends throwing up all over each other and laughing about it. I just couldn't see the humor in it, myself. I thought it was so sad that that was the best they could come up with for entertainment. Really sad. Who knows, though, maybe if I'd pickled my brain every Saturday night for a year or so, I wouldn't find myself in this current situation. I really don't believe that, Di.

Well, off the track of my main story once again. Mom seemed satisfied with all my answers to her questions. I then took my turn asking my big ones.

I asked her why in the world she and Pop took me in after my natural parents died. She looked at me in utter amazement. "You needed us, and we loved you!" Simple. Sincere. Straight forward. THE END! I guess I knew what her answer was going to be before I asked, but it was so nice to just hear it outright!

"Did you ever have second thoughts about taking me in," I then went on? "NEVER!" she shot back, looking me straight in the eye. I was convinced! (smile, deep, deep, deep, down in my heart)

I helped her do the dishes. We chatted about this and that, the way we always used to do when I'd help her in the kitchen after supper. Nothing more of real importance. Before I left, I hugged her - a little longer than usual. I kissed her on the cheek - then looked at her and kissed the other one.

I think we both felt this had been a very special time of love. That was probably my last hug for Mom - probably the best I'd ever received! That's how it should be, I think, Di. That last one should be the very best!!

6:00 PM, July 4, 1952
30 hours to go

Dear Diary,

I'm up in the attic now, Di – the unfinished section. I wonder how many wonder-filled hours I have spent up here? Many, many hundreds, I'm sure. Attics are great places, Di. They are where families store their history: the dresses Mom used to wear in the old days; the swim suit Pop used to wear (like a tee-shirt and swim trunks all combined); the big old radio with a dozen tubes in it (each six or eight inches tall; old books; and a box of love letters Pop wrote to Mom when she was in high school (I've never peeked, but I've come close!) It's so hard to think of Pop as ever having been romantic! (shake of the head, pull up bottom lip)

Pop's hunting guns are up here, now. Mom never liked them downstairs - I never liked them anywhere! The idea of killing a living thing has always turned my stomach. When I was little, I'd tramp along behind Pop as he'd go hunting. I liked being with him and being outside, but I always cringed when he'd shoot something. I hated cleaning rabbits and pheasants, but that was a part of hunting. Pop never killed an animal we didn't eat. I respected him for that. I'm sure it really did ease the meager food budget we must have had.

I still have to wonder if Pop thought I was a sissy for not becoming a hunter. He never forced the issue. He'd shoot my B-B gun with me sometimes. We'd toss cans into the air and shoot at them. I'm sure Pop never missed. Those were good times - I didn't have to be as good a shot as Pop. Those really were good times!! (dreamy smile)

Pop's old family flag is kept up here too - all folded neatly at the top of the stairs so it's easy to find. Mom taught me to name the states in order of admission to the Union by counting the stars on that old flag. It's always been special in this house - almost sacred. I never really understood how a symbol (like a flag) could become almost more sacred than the thing it stood for. I was allowed to question the government and Roosevelt and Truman, but not the Flag. Strange!

Here is my copy of *Plato's Apology*. Di, that's all about how Socrates - my hero of all hero's - justified (explained) the life he chose to live - way, way back in ancient Greece. Socrates killed himself by drinking hemlock. He spent his last day on earth visiting with his friends, revisiting his special memories, and getting things in order for when he'd be gone. That's what I'm doing now, Di. He enjoyed his last day. I'm enjoying mine, also. He really loved life - he'd never have killed himself if the government hadn't ordered his execution. That's a difference between us, I guess. No one (knowingly, at least) ordered my death.

We were alike in lots of ways, though - Socrates and me. We both loved to talk and debate and use logic. We both loved to hear what other people were thinking and to find out why. He was a sculptor, too, early in his life. I love to sculpt - even won some awards! Most everyone liked both of us - friends as well as competitors. We both had a ready wit and (like the surgeon) could keep those around us in stitches! Neither of us ever put anyone else down - not in a mean way - though we might chide others occasionally, to make a point with them. I don't know if Socrates used the pun or not. I love the pun - I know, Di, they call it the lowest form of humor, but then again, puns never hurt anyone. And, every time someone groans at them, I know they're really saying, "I wish I'd thought of that!" Good-by Socrates, my good and valued friend.

Here's my well-worn copy of Walden Pond, by Henry David Thoreau - another hero of sorts. He and Emerson were good friends. I like Emerson's writing a lot. Here is the quote from Emerson I put on a card and tacked up over my desk, so I would see it and read it every day.

Success

"To laugh often and much; to win the respect of intelligent people and the affection of children; to earn the appreciation of honest critics and endure the betrayal of false friends; to appreciate beauty, to find the best in others; to leave the world a bit better, whether by a healthy child, a garden patch or a redeemed social condition; to know even one life has breathed easier because you have lived. This is to have succeeded."

I think I've done all of that pretty well - as far as life has let me. Something must be missing, though, because I certainly don't feel successful. I should say, that although I feel successful in most of my relations with other people, I haven't been successful in my relations within myself. Does that make sense? I think so. Yes!

Here's Sigmund Freud's book, *The Interpretation of Dreams*. That really opened up a whole, new world for me - the unconscious mind and all the good and bad it can do to us. Dreams are fun to analyze, but my very favorite time is that twilight area between wakefulness and sleep - before dreams begin. I have the most fantastic images, thoughts, colors and shapes just float in and out. It's a time when many, if not most, of my great ideas hit me. I wish I could extend that time forever - then I'd probably not have to leave this way.

See this book, Di - It's a collection of short essays by Mark Twain - a great man with words and a keen observer of people. He could say so much in so few words. (I know, Di! Not one of my skills!!) My favorites in this book are his *Diary of Adam and Diary of Eve*. Funny, insightful, a bit risqué, but puts a lot of things about life into perspective. Everyone should read them (Woops! Well, if they want to!) (sheepish grin)

Just look at all these other precious books, each one filled with the wonders of man's mind and the universe. William James' psychology and philosophy books. I like what James says about reality. He says it really doesn't matter, what *real* is. The only important thing is what we *think* real is. Since we act and react to what we believe is real (or right or just or wrong), the whole idea of what might *really* be, is unimportant.

To James, the test of whether or not something is true, is whether or not it works. If it works, it's true. If it doesn't work, it's not true. The hard part of this, is that sometimes, like with religion, some parts work fine for me (giving hope, inner peace, a set of positive social values, etc.), while other parts don't work for me (makes you feel guilty, going on religious crusades and killing thousands of people who don't believe the same way, etc.). Pretty confusing. Certainly not black and white, is it?

Over here is Shakespeare. He is really hard to read until you learn the meaning of a few Old English words he used. Then it is so beautiful - so insightful. Old Billy S. was also quite the psychologist and philosopher, I think.

Oh look, Di, here are the Nursery Rhymes - Remember how some of those used to scare me to death (beg your pardon!). I'd try to get to sleep in a hurry after Mom read those to me at night, so I wouldn't just lay there seeing wolves and trolls and foreboding, dark forests. I don't believe I'd read most of those to my kids if I had any (any kids, that is, not trolls!) - not when they were really small, at least. Nursery rhymes only seem to serve adult purposes - to control little kids through fear. It's a lot like a big part of the god stuff, I guess.

Here are my first roller skates. They have six big metal washers bolted together to make each wheel. Pop made them from bits and pieces. I was so proud of them. Remember when I overhauled them in the front room and got oil all over Mom's rug. Not a happy event! She helped me learn about using soap and sawdust to remove the oil. I used it as my first science project.

Here is the special box I kept things in, back when I was three or so. Later on, I wrote a poem about it, remember.

Let's see if I can remember how it went.

My Special Box

When I was just a little boy
My Pop made me a box.
A box far better than a toy -
A box that really locks!

Well, as I grew, I came to use
It as a special place
For stuff I didn't want to lose -
Those things could not replace.

When there would come a rainy day
I'd sit there on my bed
And dump the box in disarray,
To sort my things, there spread.

That box was FULL of memories -
A rock from Jennings Brook,
Some pretty leaves from maple trees,
My very first fishhook.

A golden buckle from a belt,
The string from sweatshirt hood.
A blanket piece that I had felt,
When younger, to feel good.

A shiny nickel I had earned
From helping Pop downtown,
A poem that once I had learned,
An eye from my stuffed clown.

That box was like the diaries
That older kids wrote in.
It saved for me those memories
That told me where I'd been!

Oh, Di, you'll like this. Here are the boxes containing all

my diaries I've written in over the years. I wonder how many pages there are. Well, including the year Mom wrote down what I dictated (I didn't write well yet at four – my head knew the letters but my fingers stumbled over constructing them), and at about three pages a day, 365 days a year for thirteen years - that's roughly 15,000 pages. A lot of thoughts recorded there. A lot of memories. See how important you have been to me, Di! I could always think best about really important matters with a pen in my hand and you on my desk or in my lap. All my firsts are in those pages, Di. All my successes, all my dreams, all my happiness, all my despair. A lifetime, I guess, isn't it. A lifetime in four little boxes. (blank, empty look, I guess?)

In the corner there, are the stilts Pop and I made when I was seven or so. I worked so hard mastering them. It never entered my head that I wouldn't be able to do it, of course. Remember, Di, how I got so I could jump rope on them and even play badminton. I wrote a poem about that too. All those verses I've written are here in these files - there are thousands of them. A poem a day for over ten years - that's a minimum of 3,650. I've written about everything from love to lint - apple cobbler to cobwebs. Remember the first one I sold to the Post -

Ode To The Catsup Bottle

Slap and slap the catsup bottle!
First none'll come,
And then, a lot'll!

Remember my new improved versions of the Nursery Rhymes. Some of those were so raunchy I never showed them to anyone - except Ginny, of course. Jack and Jill - that was my favorite. I can't remember exactly how it went. I'm going to take time to try and find it ...

Sorry that took so long, Di, but I got hooked reading some of the other ones. What fun! Here's Jack and Jill.

Jack and Jill (the real scoop!)

When Jack was just a little guy,
He had the hots for Jill.
And being very, very sly,
He asked her up the hill.

She said, "The hill, whatever for?
I hope you understand,
I'm shy and ne'er alone before
With such a handsome man."

My only motive, Jack replied,
Is getting H2O
For Granny, who I keep supplied
To bathe her gouty toe.

Then Jack and Jill went up that hill -
A bucket in their hands.
And much to Jack's surprise, found Jill
Had overactive glands!

She kissed his lips and kissed his cheek.
He sat the bucket down.
His face got red! His knees got weak!
He fell and broke his crown!

Now you have learned what did take place -
Jill's passion, loose and raw.
But Jack did not get past first base
And that was Jill's one thaw!

Now, Jack and Jill are ninety-two.
Each night, old hopeful Jack,
Still slips his Jill a drop or two
Of aphrodisiac!!!!!

I can't resist putting just one more in here, Di. I hadn't even
thought of this one for years.

Little Miss Muffet

Miss Muffet was not real impressive.
Her genes, seemingly, were regressive.
She spent her long days,
Adrift in a haze,
Just being a manic depressive!

Our little blond Muffet felt lonely.
In childhood, had been an only.
No brother or sis,
Such fights she did miss.
(I'm sure they'd have laid her out pronely!)

Now what self-respecting young spider,
Would get close enough to go bite her?
This pitiful tyke,
No one really liked.
Her Mom even tried hard to hide her!

Oh, look at that mouth on Miss Muffet!
Her goal seems to be just to stuff it!
She eats curds and whey,
While sitting all day,
Which explains her stupendous big tuffet!

Well, I must run, now, Attic. Thanks for being such a safe place for me all these years. Perhaps, I could just stay up here ... No, I guess the time has come for me to leave all of you good and faithful friends who live here. You have served me well. I have arranged exciting new places for many of you to go and live now. Do as well for your new friends as you have done for me. Really, I guess, do *better* for them.

7:00 PM, July 4, 1952
29 hours to go

Dear Diary,

I was just sitting at the park watching the kids. I won't have any kids, you know, Di. I think I would have been a good father - probably an even better grandfather. Little kids like me. I wasn't sitting there for more than a minute when several of them tried to get me to pitch for both of their ball teams - seems they can't find a five-year-old arm that is accurate enough for that task this evening. I declined today. They were disappointed. That pleased me. Probably, it shouldn't have.

Mrs. Wilson came by with her new baby. She sat and we talked for a few minutes. I got to hold little Suzie. She is so tiny! Her little fingers and toes. She's bald as a cue ball. Her eyes don't go where she wants them to yet. She still smells like a baby. I wonder when that wears off? You know, Di, like the smell in a new car - one day it's just not there anymore - I wonder when it leaves a baby?

Suzie's probably the last baby I'll ever hold. It's really special to care for a baby, Di. They depend on you completely for everything and they don't even know it. Like just holding her - she depended on me not to drop her and not to let her head flip back and not to squeeze her too hard and to keep her cool enough tonight. She smiled when I tickled her cheek. I know it was probably just a reflex, but still, this tiny little human being smiled - like saying, "I trust you to take good care of me, Craig." That's a whole lot of responsibility! I'm certainly not ready for that!

I think you should have to pass a test before you can become a parent. Maybe that sounds silly to you, Di, but I mean it. At thirteen, insert a cork in all the girls and apply a rubber band to all the boys! You should have to learn all the things a parent needs to know about in order to make and raise a kid so he grows up healthy and happy and loving - curious and dependable and trusting. How do you suppose that you do that? I mean, help a child really learn all of those important things? Seems to me a lot of parents don't! Ergo, a class.

I'm really smart, and I surely don't know. See, we should all have to take some classes and pass a test first. Maybe that way kids wouldn't grow up hating themselves or others.

Maybe they wouldn't be so lazy and unconcerned about the World and their fellow man. Maybe they wouldn't be so mean to other kids who are a little different. Maybe they wouldn't find it necessary to get drunk out of their minds every Saturday night. Maybe, as adults, they'd stop and think about the long-term consequences of what they are about to do to, or say to, a youngster.

Di, I think knowing how to be a great parent is the most important thing a school should be teaching, and mine didn't even mention it once - all through school, not even once! Yes Sir, I think we should have to pass a test - only a grade of A+ passes, by the way. No corks out or rubber bands off till they earn an A+.

You know, Di, come to think of it, school didn't even really even help me learn about just plain old how to get along with others or how to like myself. Oh, when we'd misbehave, Principal Kelley would lay a few swats on our behinds, but I mean to really make an effort to help us learn how to get along better - never!!! (sad, mad, exasperated face)

You know, Di, with only a few exceptions, like Mrs. Wilson and Mrs. Heatherton, my school experience didn't even really help kids learn to love learning - can you beat that!! They made it a chore instead of a pleasure! (triple frown) I was so fortunate there. Mom and Pop loved to learn new things so much, and, early on, I got all caught up in it from them. Pop was probably the best educated 6th grade dropout ever! He read all the time. No topic he couldn't talk about knowledgeably. Every semester, he'd have my new textbooks read before I did. It's such a shame the schools, back then, didn't see how smart he was - how much potential he had. They just let him drop out and go to work at the Plant when, really, he was still a little boy. I wonder if that made him sad. He was probably frustrated all his life, wasn't he? I never really thought about that before. I wonder what Pop would have really liked to have been.

Ginny's always talking about how it is the duty of a smart guy like me to have lots and lots of children in order to make the World a better place, by passing on to it more intellectual potential. If being smart, like me, just means that it's easier to see all the horrors and impossibilities in life, then I have to disagree with her. At any rate, I guess the world will never get to know my children, and, since I've never had sex, I guess there's not even the slimmest chance for one of my strays to make his mark on the world, is there!

I hear other guys boasting about all their sexual conquests and how they've all had Sharon at one time or another (or another or another!). I once dubbed her, "Old Sharon Share Alike." (That's a sound gag, Di. It's hard to write - "share 'n share alike."). Unfortunately, that stuck. I'm sorry I did that to her. I think the other guys are mostly lying, anyway. (maybe, perhaps, possibly, who knows?) On the other hand, at eighteen and single, she has had two babies, so I suppose at least one of the guys has to be telling the truth!

I thought that having sex was one thing I really wanted to do before tomorrow night is over, but now that I'm this close, I really don't know. Frankly, I don't know how to go about it - Oh, I know how to have sex (that takes no brains, just hormones!), but I don't know how to approach a girl for sex. Maybe I'll stop by Sharon's place later on, and just see if anything comes up, so to speak.

I'd sure not want to father a child at this stage of my life. The poor baby would probably end up in an orphanage and go through life even worse off than I have. Maybe that's not such a good idea.

I always told myself I wanted to have sex for the first time with my bride on our wedding night. I gather that's how it's usually done, or is that just old-fashioned thinking? That's surely how the Church teaches. That's how Ginny says she wants it to be for her - but then Ginny's a girl, and from talking with her about sex, it appears that girls don't have this tremendous force that wells up inside of them like it does inside us guys - a force that constantly screams at us - propels us toward sexual fulfillment. Nothing else seems to matter much once that urge begins to peak. Nothing much can really stop it - delay it, perhaps, but not really stop it. Ginny really doesn't seem to have the faintest idea of what I'm talking about when I tell her about that. Girls!?

Remember back before puberty, Di, when life was so simple - though I couldn't possibly have known that at the time, of course. Girls were merely a nuisance that you had to put up with and be nice too. The adult sexual relationship was still an unknown and unfathomable concept.

Then whammo! Life was forever changed, Di. No more innocence. It was changed for the better, I presume, but it certainly complicated the over-all scheme of my universe.

Time is slipping by, Di. Time for the band concert down in the park. First time in six years I won't be playing. Sort of sad. I could have. Didn't want (or choose) to. I'll just sit up by the stone wall and listen. I need to keep on writing, anyway. I am falling way behind schedule (mildly panic-stricken look).

8:00 PM, July 4, 1952
26 hours to go

Dear Diary,
I have been listening to the concert and watching the people. It still seems that I am somewhat detached from it all. I'm sitting up on the wall along Green Street. The band has played the same songs they've played at every concert for the last ten years. The people applaud with wild appreciation (genuine!) after each one, just like they have done for as long as I can remember. Those folks who sit in their cars honk their horns instead of clapping, just like always. The little kids chase each other in and about the benches, the people, and the trees, just as little kids have always done before.

Sitting here watching, I realize it's the same event over and over. Year after year. The event doesn't change - just the participants change. Jerry is playing the clarinet part now that I used to play, and before me, that part was played by the Utley kid. It's a new batch of little kids playing chase, but the chase is the same. It's different horns on different cars, but their sound is still the same.

It's an unchanging miniature slice of human existence. The people come and go, but the traditions - the social event - remains constant. Which is real here, Dr. James, the flesh and blood people or the event? One person, more or less - how does it matter? The band doesn't miss my fingers and my arms and my lungs - it just plays on. The game of chase doesn't need my young little legs - it just joyously continues. The audience doesn't need my hands to applaud - it does just fine without me. It all goes on just fine without me. We're all replaceable, Di - expendable - if you will. If I had never been in Springfield, it all still would have gone on just the same. There would have been other legs, other fingers, other hands.

There is one more thing, however, that absolutely requires my participation, Di. Are birth and death all that is real Dr. James? Is everything in between just illusion?

I must stop this line of thinking. I've just, this morning, left my depression behind - let's not reinstate it now! I don't want to be depressed at the end. (That last statement must be, somehow, humorous! This has been a very weird entry Di!)

9:00 PM, July 4, 1952
27 hours to go

Dear Diary,

During the last part of the concert, I went over to the big sandbox in the park. There were a few little kids still there. We built one huge sandcastle together. Everybody helped - the six-year olds - the ten year olds - everybody. We had a great time!

They kept asking, "How shall we do it?" "What's it supposed to look like when it's done?" Questions I've always asked myself about me, Di. You know what I told those kids, Di? I said, "Just do it anyway that feels right - just don't bother anybody else's part." I said, "Nobody knows how it's supposed to look until it's finished - then we'll know."

Can you believe that I said those things, Di - Me, old plan-everything-down-to-the-last-detail-Craig? What fun! What absolutely glorious fun!! No plan - just go at it! It ended up about four feet high and must have been six feet square.

We talked a lot while we worked - no, while we played - see, everything I do - even play - I have always thought of as work - until tonight. What a sense of freedom! We were our only judges and we thought it was the most wonderful sandcastle ever built! And so, it *really* was. Thank you, Dr.

James. It had a moat that Benny built. Some tiny bridges that Jake made. Perry did the wall. I did the main big tower. My tower was for my beautiful maiden to live in. Jake and Perry put their fingers down their throat at the thought of that. I would have wanted to do that, too, at there age - good going guys! Kids should be kids, just the way kids are supposed to be kids!

I noticed, later, that we hadn't put any entrances through the wall. I didn't mention it. Seemed quite secure and safe that way.

Somewhere along the way, Benny asked me what I thought he ought to be when he grew up. He liked digging the moat, so he thought he might be a ditch digger. Probably not so far from the likely outcome for poor, slow, little Benny. I told him to stop worrying about what was going to be fifteen years from now - that will come along on its own. That instead, he should just think about who he wants to be today, and then try his best to just be exactly that six-year-old person.

What do you think of that advice, Di? Pretty good, I'd say! I don't know where it came from - just out of the blue. I guess it's too late for me to follow it. I've just grown up too different - I mean, I just think about myself and everything too differently from that. Obviously, the way I've thought about living has been wrong - look at me here - twenty-six hours away from being seventeen - twenty-six hours away from pulling the plug. I can give everybody else such good advice. Why can't I do the same for myself, Di? Why?

For some reason, I asked them how long it had been since they had told each of their family members that they loved them and really meant it. There's a difference, you know, Di, between saying, "Love ya," to Mom as I run out the door, and really meaning it - really stopping to think about what it means. Too often we don't think about the meaning behind the words we say. Even the most important ones like to believe they are truly – sincerely – loved.

I should have asked them how often they tell themselves that they love themselves. I guess they are too young yet to really understand that. I don't know when I stopped loving myself. Gradually, I guess. I still love others a whole lot. I know I really hated my little boy's body back when I entered

High School at nine. That was powered by the unnatural situation. When I did finally get a grown-up model, I guess that was mostly okay - a least I always thought it should be. It's a great body for an athlete. That's what Parson told me at fourteen - "God has given you the body of a champion, Craig, you must use it so He'll be proud of you." That may be the moment I began hating my great, new, grown-up body. Even my body became the source of way too much responsibility - and, this time, to GOD, no less. (very sad face)

Once I put that god stuff on the back burner - which was very soon after puberty pounced on me - I began to get it all worked out. (I'm not suggesting that other people should give up on this god idea, understand. I'm just saying *for me* it made my universe make much more sense without it.)

Well, I'm wandering off the track again. I think I learned to hate myself a little more each time I was - what shall I call it - super-successful. For example, I could handle a few A's, but when I realized at ten, that I'd never made anything but A's, that old familiar pressure welled up inside me again. Now, I had set another precedent I had to live up to. Everybody expected Craig to make all A's. (I suppose they had for a long time, but I just hadn't realized it yet.) I really hated to let other people down.

A lot of the fun of learning stopped at that point. Before, I'd really just do the assignments because I loved to have the chance to learn new things. I never thought much about grades. Possibly never. From ten on, however, I felt I first had to master the assignments; only then could I go ahead and learn the things I wanted to. I hated that, and I hated me for buying into it!

When Perry was making the wall tonight, a section of it crumbled, and he was ready to give up. "I can't do this damn thing right," he screamed! "I quit!" I told him if we'd all quit the first time we had a problem, we'd all just be sitting around twiddling our thumbs while we watched the world fall apart around us. I told him that the way we learn is to think about our mistakes and then try it some different way the next time. After a few tries, we find a way that works.

I dried his tears on my tee shirt (dirty as it was, it was still cleaner than poor little neglected Perry's face). We started building again. Later on, Perry sat on a section of his wall on purpose so he could say, "I guess I'll just have to rest a different way next time." We laughed. I chased him down, tackled him out in the grass, and tickled him up one side and down the other. He kicked and laughed and smiled and enjoyed it so much! (There is not much fun in his home-life.) Finally, we tired and just lay there in the cool grass for a moment - close together - breathing hard through our broad smiles. "I love you, Craigy," he whispered in his soft, high pitched little six-year-old voice. I turned my head and looked at him. "I love you, too, Perry, just the way you are tonight." Then, it was back to the castle.

It was a great time. I really didn't want that to end! It was like being a little kid again, emotionally, but all grown up, intellectually. Why not? I could probably stick around if there were just a place like that for me. (Where's Peter Pan's, Never-Never Land when you need it?) (smile)

I used to worry a bit about why I liked to spend so much time with little kids. I thought I was a pedophile, until I really understood the term. No Way! I've finally figured out why I do enjoy kids so much though.

In many ways, of course, I never was a little kid. That's not what I'm talking about here. First of all, little kids - say up to about ten years old - are so honest. They tell it just the way they see it. They ask right out the real questions that pop into their minds. They don't run their questions or answers or other thoughts through a censor first to see if there's any reason not to say it or ask it. You can just count on them (much to their parent's chagrin, sometimes!), to be straight with you - like the Tom Mix Straight Shooters on radio.

By the time we hit our teens, honesty doesn't seem to count much. It's more, "What am I expected to say?" "How am I expected to answer?" "What's going to be acceptable here?" "What will get me what I want right now.?" It's not so much that we teenagers set out to lie - we just have to filter everything through our will-it-play-okay-with-whomever-is-around-right-now censor.

And another thing about little kids - they just revel in life. They're out to enjoy every experience that comes along - swinging high, rolling in the grass, seeing the dead bird, helping mow the grass, taking a bath, going for a ride, watching the parade, climbing a tree, playing dress-up, digging a hole, playing chase - even building a sand castle! (After we finished, Perry asked, "What is a sandcastle, anyway?)

They really do put themselves into it - so innocently, uninhibited, oblivious to anything but the moment - the experience - the activity - the feelings. Now, I know, Di, we can't all be that way all the time - or can (could) we? Why not, I wonder? I guess I was a lot that way as a little boy, after all. Interesting to think about. Anyway, I really do appreciate seeing that vigorous involvement in every aspect of life. It only seems to exist, anymore, in little kids.

The third reason I'm taken with little kids has to do with how eager they are to learn new things - to try new things - to think about new things. It seems to me that by high school age, most kids have lost a lot of that eagerness. Many lose it even earlier - Harley, for example. A few of us don't. The last act I want to perform before I die, is to learn one last new thing. In my back pocket I have a pamphlet about Molecular Theory – that should be new.

Where does that great inquisitiveness and openness and intense involvement go? Why does it leave? What could we do to prevent it from seeping away? How can we put it back? (or can we?) How can we help those who have lost it realize how much they are missing - realize how much they need it - find out how to retrieve it?
I Have to run, Fireworks over at Billy's.

10:00 PM, July 4, 1952
26 hours to go

Dear Diary,
    I spent most of this hour at Billy's. Like usual, he and John and I pooled our fireworks and shot them off there in the empty lot. It was like we were little kids again. What fun! So silly! Nothing serious! Many memories! ("Do you remember the year we...") We were lucky we hadn't killed one another! It was like a pocket in time - six or sixteen - it made no difference. It was every night of every 4th of July. We shot off

our fireworks just as we had done since time (for us) began. Earlier, I thought maybe we'd get a chance to talk seriously, but that wasn't on the menu tonight.

I never had much money to spend on fireworks, but they understood that, and were always more than willing to share everything equally. Tonight, when I arrived with a basket full, they could hardly believe it. "Close out your bank account, Craigy?" (If they had only known!)

Tonight, we had skyrockets and Roman candles and sparklers and pinwheels and, of course, firecrackers. I had never before had enough firecrackers that I felt like I could light a whole pack at once and hear that wonderful rat-a-tat-tat - see them jumping from here to there and back again! Well tonight was different, Di! Five packs, I lit that way!

We blew up ant hills, blew bottles to smithereens, frightened the feces out of two inquisitive squirrels, and scorched each other's Levis. We wrestled and rolled in the grass. We laughed till we cried. It truly was, that 4th of July, shared once again by The Three Musketeers of Springfield. We were no age at all tonight. We were just the greatest friends that had ever been. I love them both so much - but could never tell them that out loud. I think tonight, though, without words, we reaffirmed that loving bond we have shared so long. Thanks guys!

They are good people, Billy and John. John's the patriot. Billy's the lover. I was the dreamer. A grand combination. It has worked so very well. Oh, we disagreed and got mad and stomped around a lot at each other's expense from time to time, but through it all, we have always known that we belonged together. They will miss me. I'm so sorry, guys.

John will probably become a general, someday. Billy - who knows - such a free-spirited person - Perhaps just a wonderful father and husband (Preferably, not in that order!) Being a family man is not a bad way to spend a lifetime, Billy. Me, I'll be a memory - a very good one, I hope - a part of their consciences - a part of their dreams - a part of their everlasting childhood. Good by, dear friends.

11:00 PM, July 4, 1952

25 hours left

Dear Diary,
What do you suppose most people want out of life, Di? I was thinking about that on the way back here to my room from Billy's. What have the three of us been trying to find - moment by moment, I mean. Just day by day - nothing ultimate here. Just the little things. What have we tried to find?

Laughs, a good time - that seems important to most everybody. Like tonight, we all three tried hard to keep each other in stitches, and we did! Some of that was the old, "I can top your best," routine, but together we pursued laughter as if it were a positive end, in and of itself, or, perhaps, was it really just an attempt to keep sadness from creeping in? Fill the heart with laughs so there is no room for despair? Me, partly, probably. Them, I really don't know for sure. I can't imagine anyone living to be their age and not have some sadness or unresolved something.

Entertainment - I've always assumed that people sought this. I've spent my life doing my bit to entertain everyone - all the time - everywhere - ad nauseam! I suppose it's an escape for some and a pursuit for others. I mean, some are chasing pleasure, while others are running away from pain.

Music - A lot like laughter and entertainment, I guess. Most everyone enjoys music. It comes in all varieties to please all sorts of tastes.

Thinking about just these three - do you realize how even these things, which all seem to be intended to lift our spirits, are also, the basis of such gosh awful arguments and disagreements - especially between the generations! What kind of jokes may I laugh at - clean or mildly shady or downright dirty? See, most grown ups will tell me that laughter is only okay (good, right) when it is provoked by certain kinds of acceptable stimuli. That it is bad when caused by others. (furrowed brow)

Entertainment is the same way, Isn't it? It's Okay for me to be entertained by scantily clad girls, dancing around, swinging their lovely bodies this way and that, when it's called ballet, but not when nearly the same thing takes place in a Hoochie Coochie parlor - very strange! High class erotic stimulation vs. low class, I guess.

And music - Well, need I really expound on music? Church music, classical music, popular music, old-timer's music, dance-band music, fast dance music, slow dance music, jazz. Seems like everybody likes some and hates others. The older generation never seems to like (or even approve of) the younger generation's choice. Some folks go so far as to say some music is right and some music is wrong. Interesting! I suppose, though, I am guilty of that myself, sometimes. (I hate Mom and Pop's old-time records and, on occasion, have told them so!) (frown - I think?).

What else do we seek? Status or acceptance - it's hard for me to separate those two. Neither one is a general term though, Di. They both can be very specific. I can't just try to be accepted by everyone, you see. If I want to be accepted by the band members, there is one set of things I must do - things that would not in any way lead to acceptance by, say, the football squad. And neither of those two sets of required behaviors would get me anywhere with the kids who hang out at the roller rink. What's more, each of those groups - at least the core, die-hard members of each group - really believe that to be their way is right, and to be any other way is to be wrong or at least stupid. All these mini-groups - mini-value systems - mini-allegiances - mini-prejudices - mini-suspicions. It's a wonder society holds together at all, isn't it, Di? With all of my interests and skills, I've needed to be accepted by a lot of different groups - It's been so hard - a terrible struggle - juggle - sometimes.

Another area that lots and lots of people pursue is the accumulation of things - as if things make you happy. They give us pleasure, perhaps, but momentary pleasures in no way add up to happiness. Apples and oranges, like they say. I'm not sure what happiness is, I guess. I've just seen so many folks who have all kinds of possessions (things), and yet still feel really miserable. Therefore, as Socrates would deduce, "*Things* cannot be the source of happiness."

I do many things that are pleasurable to me - like being with Billy and John tonight, playing my clarinet, sculpting, running, swimming, dating, kissing, reading - but I'm still a terribly (terminally) unhappy person. For me, I suppose, I was truly happiest when I was involved in the process of making something or creating a new thought or constructing a new poem or story. Happiness was in the process, more than in the finished product or the possession (thing) if you will. I am pleased with a lot of what I have written, for example, but the happiness part is attached back in the creating of it. Does that make sense? I guess for me the process of living has stopped being that kind of a happiness-producing process.

Too Sad - move on!

Let's see. What else do I seek - Girls! All the time we guys seek girls - girls to talk to, girls to look at, girls to be with, girls to kiss, and on down the obvious choices. Girls seem to be into most of these same things about guys - at least that's the way it appears when I talk with Ginny.

It sure seems to me that I spend an incredible amount of time thinking about girls - every day - heck, every hour - just thinking about girls!! Maybe Freud's right - all human behaviors are motivated by sex. Why do I want to be good looking? Certainly not for John! Why do I worry about my complexion? Billy could sure care less! Nice clothes? Personality? A gorgeous car someday? A well-developed body? Money? Status? - Yup! All, (or at least mostly) to get the attention of girls! Maybe it is puberty that is the culprit responsible for the downfall of the "love of learning and the pursuit of excellence" that I spoke of awhile back! (smile) (smile again) (frown) Egghead's just don't usually end up with the Home Coming Queen on their arm, now, do they - we? Sad commentary!

You know, Di, I really think, even here in peaceful little Springfield, in the center of our big and powerful USA, that a lot of us still are seeking safety every single day. I mean, I want to be strong and tough and able to protect myself. I don't want any other guys to be able to take me in a fight. I really do think about this, Di. I lift weights and I wrestle with the guys - always with this idea in the back of my mind - self-protection. I do all this, and yet, nobody ever gets beat up in Springfield; nobody ever gets threatened. Nobody gets robbed here. Heck, we don't even have house keys - nobody around here has them. So, why do I expend so much energy trying to keep safe and to be tough? We guys all do this same thing. Maybe it's an instinct left over from our distant Cave Man past (smile) - like when a dog turns around and around before lying down. Even though I really know I am safe here, I also really feel that I am not! Intriguing! Scary! Senseless? Bothersome, at least!

Then, Di, there is that one very special thing we all search for - or later wish we had - that one thing that spells out what talents or skills we really possess - our Job. When small, being a good bike rider, a good racer, rope jumper, tree climber - those things seemed to suffice. Then, later on, it becomes a search through things like being a good student, athlete, artist, musician, bully, talker, lover, salesman and so on. That's about as far as I am, I guess.

I'm not at all sure what comes next. To select just one of all those fields and pursue it, I suppose. That's what every successful adult seems to do. How do you choose, when you have so many real options and so many real interests like I do? That really is my big question, I guess. The only advice adults will ever give me is the old standard; "You are the only one who can figure that one out, Craig!" I hate myself for having so many options. I don't want to have to choose just one. It isn't fair to have to. I hate it! I hate it!! I hate it!!! (By that I mean, "*I hate it*," just in case you missed it, Di!)

We also all pursue love, I think, but I won't talk about it here. Love is a topic that permeates most everything I am writing about. Hard to separate out from all the other topics.

Looks like this last 4th of July has come to an end, Di. I see it's midnight. I need a snack. Guess I'll raid the icebox. Be back shortly.

12:00 Midnight, July 4, 1952
24 hours left

Dear Diary,
Exactly one day left, Di. Tomorrow at this time it will all be over. I have no misgivings about it. No fear, really. More intrigued and exhilarated right now than fearful. I do wonder though ... Never mind.
After it's all over, what will I have left behind? I hope it's

more than a tombstone and my name carved on the oak tree up on the hill. I want my tombstone to read, "He Tried." I *have* tried, you know, Di. I really have tried! It's strange, I could always figure everything out - everything except life or how I could fit into it.

I hope I am leaving behind some really good memories for lots and lots of people. We've had some really good times - these townspeople and me. The Old Timers will never forget, I'm sure, that day when I was four, and I danced a jig in the talent show. I put myself into it with such gusto, my pants fell down. I kept right on jigging. Mom finally rescued me (or the audience - I'm not sure which!). For years, the morning coffee drinkers down at the cafe called me "Jig".

And that Sunday morning at church - the day after I got my Mohawk haircut to spite Pop - Pop gave the lay message. He chose race relations as his topic. I remember word for word how he began: "Although treating all races and groups of people with friendship and respect is always important, I find it even more crucial today - now that I have a young Indian lad living in my home." The congregation actually laughed out loud, Di. - I hadn't heard so much as a chuckle during a church service as long as I'd been attending - and, at me they broke their long-standing silence and laughed out loud! Total and complete embarrassment!

It presents an appropriate opportunity to say how proud I have been of Pop. Did you know, Di, that he was the first Negro to ever be a Deacon in the Church of the Brethren — the very first. That may have said more about the church elders than it did about dad — the day, the age, the rampant prejudice of the day. There was no better man, I didn't mean that.

Remember when I was fifteen, and I won the State Invitational Swimming Marathon - a twenty-hour swim for distance. Everybody met our car at the edge of town and walked along side with congratulation signs, cheering all the way to the school. That was a highlight for me - I hope they can remember it that way too.

Of course, they'll all remember with pleasure, I'm sure, that day, late in May, five years ago, now, when, at eleven years of age, I was the youngest High School graduate ever in the state. The Governor came to hand me my diploma. I only remember the sadness in my own heart because I'd be leaving my friends, and the fear of the big unknown - College at twelve!

I guess, all in all, the townspeople will remember me as a nice person who tried his best to make life better for those around him. I'm proud of that, and yet at the same time, I hate it SO much. If I had just been able to be a nice guy because I had wanted to, that would have been great. But I felt I had to be a nice guy because everyone gave me the impression that I owed it to them for the many kindnesses they had bestowed on me, the poor little orphan kid from the wrong end of town with the wrong color parents. They didn't really say it in so many words (usually), but I felt that it was always implied. It's one of the only two things that ever really made me genuinely, gut deep, mad when I was younger.

Sometimes, when other kids would get in trouble, I'd envy them so - wish it could have been me. Of course, it seldom was, so I'll be remembered as, "Good old Craigy Franklin, the sandy-headed kid with the perpetual grin." I guess not really a bad way to be remembered. When they realize that I killed myself, they will ask: "What went wrong with him?" They'll never ask the right question, "Where did we go wrong with him?" I guess that's okay - I'm not looking to heap guilt on anybody through this thing. Anyway, I should have been able to handle it!

I think I've made Mom and Pop's life better. I know I was a burden to them financially, and often, I'm afraid, emotionally, also - but when all is balanced out, I think I brought them much more joy and pride and sense of accomplishment than they would have ever experienced without me. I certainly hope so. That's how it is when you have kids, Di. They are both a pain and a joy. Parents who truly understand that are great for their kids - Parents who don't, are devastating for them. Thank goodness, Mom and Pop understood! I hope those joys will eventually help Mom overcome the positively terrible grief that I am about to inflict on her. (saddest face imaginable - lots of tears - wet page)

Maybe someday, someone will find and publish the two manuscripts I titled, A Big Kid's Letters To Little Kids, and Stuff Kids Wish Parents Remembered About Being Kids. Maybe those can go on helping folks even after I'm gone. Maybe this diary will help someone understand something that will prevent them from having to follow in my despicable (lousy) footsteps. I know I am being a terrible model, but I'm sick to death of always having to be the model. 'Sick to death' - that pretty well says it, Di. Maybe someone will read you, though, Di, and understand how precious and wonderful life can be, when you don't let yourself get on the wrong track - and stay there too long. I hope no other kid ever finds that he can't ask for help because that would tarnish his image as being perfect. UGH!

I'm writing these pages, of course, in the hope they will somehow, someday, be helpful to someone. I hope I can, through these pages, reach out across time and really help somebody. You see, life has tried it's best to be good to me. It really has. I just couldn't make it work - I couldn't accept the cards it dealt. I know, to most folks, my hand looks like all aces. Why has it seemed to me to be mostly jokers?

But, back to my legacy. What else do I leave behind? It seems that mostly, I just have memories to leave for others. I've built a lot of memories for the people in this little town. I suppose memories are really better than monuments. They may not last as long, but they are more meaningful while they do last. A building named after someone - or a statue - could just as well have any name on it if you don't really know about that person. When people have good memories left to them they remain attached to that person forever. I think I have left good memories.

My poems - corny verses, really, I suppose. Perhaps they will bring joy or meaning to someone's life someday. That would be so nice! I have surely enjoyed writing them. My college English prof says they'll never be known as great because of the mundane, everyday topics I write about - like: hiccups, lint, catsup, clouds, math, spelling bees, snowflakes, cobwebs, monsters, penmanship, chewing gum, paper clips, naps, storms, germs, warts, beds, crying, car sickness, ear aches - well, Di, you get the drift. Prof. says to be memorable a poem must sing the praises of love or beauty.

I guess at sixteen, I still don't know very much about love, do I, Di? - Not romantic love anyway. I think I have been a very loving person in the general sense, and I have most certainly, "fallen in love" with the physical beauty of dozens and dozens of girls, but I really haven't known the wonders of true romantic love. (Have I?)

But, anyway, I hope my poems will bring smiles to the faces, and fond memories to the hearts of those who may read them. If they never become well known, that's fine, too. At least that way, no poor, uninterested, captive, school kids will ever have to agonize over memorizing them or, worse still, search them for the 'hidden meaning of the author.' (But, just on the chance they might have to be read in school someday, School Kids everywhere take note. The only intended meanings in my poems are these: It is important to be able to laugh at your own foibles, to love yourself and others with all your being, and to look at your World from unique, unconventional angles in order to make sure you don't miss a thing! Appreciate the little stuff.)

I guess the most important of all those messages, is to learn how to love yourself - I mean really love yourself. That's the one I sure messed up on. When you love yourself, it seems that it doesn't matter so deeply when you are criticized, or when others don't understand you, or when life takes an unexpected or unpleasant turn. You can tell yourself, "I know I'm just fine, regardless of what others may be thinking or saying right now." To love yourself, allows you to pursue integrity - a kind of self-respect - I think, Di. I think that only when you love yourself, can you truly be at peace inside. I was like that as a kid. I wonder how I screwed that up so badly. All I ever needed was to be able to say, "Craigy, you are great. You are helpful and want the best for others. If all people believed and behaved like you do, the world would be a super great place for every last one of us."

It's fascinating, Di, this feeling I have been having in my 'heart' as I have been writing this entry. It is as if I really do love the person who may be reading this, even years from now - someone I'll never meet - never get to know - someone who may not even be born yet. WOW! I feel as though that person is my friend and that I am theirs. I guess when one truly does love the entire Family of Man, as I have always tried to do, time, like race and creed, is irrelevant - I really can love you, my reader - my friend - my dear, dear young friend.

I do so wish that I could tell you just exactly how to go about loving yourself - what a legacy that would be! There's bound to be a way. I implore you to keep looking - to keep searching. Please, my friend, you must keep searching!

Who am I talking to, Di? All kids everywhere in every time, or maybe, just to myself? Perhaps we are really the same.

I'm just beat, Di. I'm going to take a nap. Don't go away. (smile, yawn, stretch)

1:00 AM, July 5, 1952
23 hours left

Dear Diary,

I just slept this hour. Feel much better now. I didn't count on needing so much sleep. All this thinking seems to be sapping my energy. That's Okay, I'm still fairly close to being on schedule.
2:00 AM, July 5, 1952
22 hours left

Dear Diary,

It's two AM, Di. I'm just sitting here in the window seat. This will be my last night here in my comfortable, little attic room. How many times have you and I done this together, right here? It's a great night out - warm and dry, just a little breeze coming in through the window. I'll go prowl around a bit in a little while. I still want to get up to the cemetery, but I'll wait until dawn, for that.

I had set this time aside here, in the wee hours of the morning, to think and write about my special memories. When I made up this outline, I remember thinking I'd use this time to look back on all my 'great' accomplishments, but now, that's not what comes to mind at all - Funny! I've just been staring out into the black sky seeing images about growing up poor, here with Mom and Pop and - get this - how really great it all was. It's true, though, Di, for me, growing up money-poor with Mom and Pop to help me understand about it, *was* really great!

It's strange. though, Harley also grew up poor, but he hates it - of course, he hates everything and everybody. I wonder why we became so different. We are both only kids; both have older, unschooled parents; attended the same school; same teachers; belonged to the same church; and though he's not a certified genius, he has plenty on the ball, intellectually, if he'd ever decide to use it.

I think Harley's family felt the world owed them. I'm not sure why. I don't really know much about their background, I guess. But they'll take and take and take, and seldom offer thanks. They stay mostly to themselves. Harley's been in trouble all his life - stealing, destroying property, fighting - he even set fire to the church when he got mad at his folks for trying to force him to go to Sunday School. He's always failed in school - he flunked almost as often as I got skipped ahead. We used to joke that Harley was the only 4th grader in history who could grow a moustache! (I was probably the only college sophomore, who couldn't!)

I remember trying to get close to him once (at Parson's request!). He hated me - never said why - seemed, though, because he saw me as successful – 'lucky,' Harley called it. I guess he had learned to just wait around for fate to do its thing, and, when it didn't bless him with what he wanted, he became bitter and spiteful. He'd steal toys and bikes and such, even though he knew he'd be caught. (Stolen property is never difficult to trace here in Springfield - Harley's the only one in town who has stolen anything in years.) Then, he'd destroy what he had taken before it could be returned to its owner. When things start going bad, I guess it's really hard to hang in there. I feel bad for Harley - he'll end up in jail, or worse, and I don't have a clue how to prevent it - I gather no one else does either, because, most certainly, nothing is being done about it. Such a waste. (major frown)

By contrast, my 'poor' life, has been great! (I think I've said that a few times before.) We were only ever poor in terms of money and certain 'things' - never poor in frame of mind or in love or in companionship. Mom and Pop taught me well, about the value and rewards of honest work - and when there was no work at home, the value of going out and being helpful to others - or of dreaming great dreams - or of planning, of reading, of learning. Di, you remember, how, at every evening meal we'd play the game Mom called, 'Think a thought that's never been thought before'? We'd each try to top the others with something we felt pretty sure no one else in all of eternity had ever before thought. What wise folks to expand my thinking skills in that way.

When I was small, many of my "new thoughts" were, of course, not new to the world of thought, but they were new as far as I could have known. Then, later, they became truly unique - sometimes funny, sometimes frightening, always stimulating. I have to thank Mom and Pop for helping me dream - for helping me to see things from unique and new perspectives - to never just accept and be satisfied with the way things appear on the surface. Not to accept the status quo. To never give up just because someone else says it can't be done. What riches they bestowed upon me! (Why is all of that failing me now?)

Pop taught me never to just sit around being 'bored' - sitting around was fine if that was my purpose - but never, ever say, 'I'm bored!' There were always hundreds of things to do if you just set your mind to finding them. For example, there were always books just filled with new things to learn about, other folks who needed a helping hand, gadgets that needed to be invented, poems that needed to be written, old folks and sick folks who needed a visit, ball games that needed to be played, songs just waiting to be composed, and on and on and on!
Mom and Pop took 'parenting' very seriously. I know they talked daily about me and things they needed to be doing or thinking about for me. I wonder if all parents make time in their lives to make such constant assessments and readjust their plans. The best one's do, I'm sure.

I got my first steady job when I was ten. Remember, Di. Two hours every evening cleaning up Miss Molly's beauty shop. At age eleven, I added two more hours each day, early in the morning, helping Mr. Elzer in the grocery store. By the time I was thirteen, I was working twenty hours a week and carrying a double load at college. I was always so happy for a new opportunity to work. I was also in the city band, on the community swimming team, debate club, and I even had a swing band of my own for two years (locally referred to as, *Pip*

72

and his Squeaks.) Well, you know, Di. I kept busy, stimulated and productive. I found time to write a little every day, also. It's been a really busy life - that part has been fine!

You know, Mom and Pop also taught me about *precious* - a concept I think Harley, and those like him, may not grasp. Nothing was ever precious to him. When something is precious to you, you protect it, treasure it, you're proud of it, you want to spend time with it, you can understand how others feel when something is precious to them. My family was precious to me - Harley's was not precious to him. Gaining new knowledge was made to be precious to me - not to Harley. Art and music were made precious to me, but Harley had no appreciation for those things at all. He is missing so much. The ability to create new ideas, new gadgets, new approaches - these were all made precious to me - not so, for poor Harley. Friends, I guess really, people, that is, human life in general, was certainly made very precious to me. We always did whatever we could to improve the lot of others, whether we knew them well (like here in town) or not (like in France or Belgium after the war). My family just really wanted to help! Poor Harley - he'd just as soon snuff out the life of anyone who crossed him or had what he wanted. (He hasn't to my knowledge.)

Certain possessions were made precious to me also. Okay, not the expensive things, or the newest fads, or the "keeping up with the Jones's" sort of possessions, but things of really special value. There were the presents from special people (the lunch box from Mrs. Stevens); the things I had worked hard to earn for myself (my watch); the things that marked those long awaited beginnings of new eras in my life (my first long summer pants); and especially, to value those things that are precious to others, even though not particularly to me (Mom's sewing machine, Pop's shotguns).

Perhaps, since Harley never learned to see things in his own life as being precious, he was unable to understand how they could come to be precious to others. He could destroy other people's things without a twinge of guilt. Harley probably doesn't even possess the emotion (or skill) of empathy. I'll bet that without this sense of preciousness first, it is nearly impossible to develop that ability to feel how others feel, and without that, one has no chance of surviving in social relationships. WOW! I've never thought that thought before! I'm sure it's not one of those "first time ever thoughts," but it was the first time I have ever put it all together in just that way. These times of discovery always send a rush of excitement through my whole being. I wish so that everyone could get this excited over their own wonder-filled thoughts!

It is so odd to me, perhaps sad to me, that I have this monumental understanding of precious, and yet I have never been able to put myself into that category. I know I have been precious to Mom and Pop and to many others, but I've never been able to be precious to ME. Right now - maybe always - that is really all that IS important. Oh, if I could only be precious to myself! I suppose it takes a far better man than I am, though, to believe that someone, who you hate as much as I hate myself, is a precious human being. (Blank, empty, desperate stare)

3:00 AM, July 5, 1952
21 hours left

Dear Diary,

Time slips by so fast. It's already three in the morning. Well, I'm not finished remembering yet, so I'll just continue.

Pop always said that little minds talk about people and things, and that big minds talk about ideas and processes. I think he meant that things like gossiping about who is doing or getting what, is limiting one's capacity to use their mind, and that talking about ideas such as ways to improve the quality of life, for example, would indicate a mind-building, mind-expanding experience.

I think that's why I disliked so many teachers' approach to instructing - they just stressed the petty little things, like who did what and when, for example, in history. They seldom ever asked (or taught) why or how or why do you suppose, type questions - Like, "How would Springfield probably be different today, if Benjamin Franklin (no relation, by the way!) had never lived?" Now there is one that could keep a mind busy for weeks and weeks. It would teach us how to think and reason and use logic and to make and test historic hypotheses. It would really require that we knew Franklin's role in our history, and about his contemporaries and what their tendencies would have been had Franklin not been around. Better yet, perhaps, "How would Springfield be different if *you* had not lived here?" See how that could drive it home - make you consider your place and relevance in and to society. But few teachers seemed to be concerned about making us critical thinkers and students who would be better able to take the facts (which are all available in books, anyway, so why clog our brains with them?) and manipulate them in meaningful and personally helpful ways

Oh, I'll give them the point that there are some facts we really do need to know, but to just stop there and think that they, the teachers, have done anything greater than any sensible 8th grade graduate, directing the same class, couldn't do, is ludicrous! (frown of all frowns)

I am truly afraid our educational system is building a generation of 'small minds.' Who will think the next great new thoughts? How are the big minds going to develop? It's terrible to think we have to develop our own mind's capacity to think, outside of school, if it really is to develop. (an even bigger frown than the frown of all frowns just above)

I'm jumping around - not my usual degree of good organization. I keep thinking more about the contrast between Harley and me. One other big difference, I think - ever since I can remember, I was told by the important adults around me, that I was one of the good guys in the World. Somewhere along the line I obviously bought into that, because look at me - I've spent the last twelve or thirteen years going about my world being 'one of the good guys.' (Not easy, by the way! But rewarding!) I guess I lived up to those grownups' descriptions (expectations, really, huh?).

The first thing that I ever remember hearing Mrs. Anderson say about her son, Harley, was one day when we were about five, I guess. He and I had gotten into some little disagreement (a 'driving one another's faces into the gravel' type disagreement, actually!) She said to my Mom something like, "Well, you know Harley - he's no good - just like his Dad and brother." If Harley learned that he was expected to be no good, in the same way I learned I was supposed to be very good, I guess then we have both just played out our assigned roles, haven't we - him the bad guy and me the good guy. (quizzical frown)

I wonder - do you suppose we really do get assigned our roles that early? Do we have any control over them ourselves? In psychology, there has been a raging controversy about how much influence our inherited traits have over us, compared with the amount our upbringing has to do with it. In both cases, however, they seem to be saying that we, as individual human beings, really don't have much control over how we turn out. I don't want to believe that! I want to think there are things we can all do (well, most people, anyway) to change ourselves for the better. On the other hand, I've tried so hard to find a way to be happy about myself, and I have certainly not been able to change that. Maybe we are predestined to turn out certain ways, regardless of what we want or do or think.

That's really quite depressing, isn't it? Here I sit, Di, believing that others must have the power within themselves to change for the better, but I don't have that power within me. Makes no sense, I know. I used to love quandaries like this one - things that seemed to be so opposed - and then to find ways of resolving them. Well, I've worked on this one about myself quite diligently and intensely for over a year now, and obviously I have been unsuccessful. Today - my last day - I find myself completely worn out from thinking about it so much. Maybe each person is given just so many thoughts to think in his lifetime, and I've already used up all of mine. That's ridiculous, of course. Let's leave that one alone for a while.

What other special memories do I have? Let's try to be less complicated - less thoughtful - more down to Earth.

Sunday afternoons were always the time we did things for others - did it as a family, usually. Mow the old folks' yards, wash their windows, clean their houses, clean up the city park, plant trees or flowers, keep walks shoveled in the winter. Sometimes, we'd just go visit folks who couldn't get out, or who didn't seem to have any other friends.

Near Christmas time, of course, we'd spend more time at home, all secretly making each other's presents. I'm glad we never bought presents for each other - making something was such a special process - it was a gift of ourselves, and that is the only real gift of love. The presents weren't expected to be beautiful or expensive - they just had to be from our heart.

I grew up relishing opportunities to do nice things for others. Nothing gives me a greater kick than knowing someone else is happier or better off or likes himself a little bit better because of something I did or made or said. (Huge smile, ear to ear)

Wish I could do the same for myself. Where did that go wrong, Di? Why can't I make myself feel good, content, happy, deep down inside where it really matters? What went wrong? Other people tell me I'm a great guy in dozens of different ways every day. Why don't I believe them, Di? Have I learned that I'm not supposed to be happy, but instead to just feel beholding to everyone else (in the whole World, it seems!)? Do I see myself as such a millstone around everyone else's neck that I'm convinced that I am more trouble to them than I'm worth? If others won't say that out loud, do I then have to say it to myself? Perhaps, I've always been too self-sufficient, or at least made it seem that way to others, so they never thought I needed reassurance, consoling, assistance, compassion or help! I'm afraid that they were dead wrong! (Not Ginny or Mom or Pop, of course.)

I may have let words veer me off course there. I really do believe I am a good person. That's not what this is all about. It's about knowing that no matter how talented I may be, I will never be able to live up to the expectations other people have for me. Why do I have to live for everybody else? Why can't I just live my life my way, doing what I want to do, for myself, and just accept however it turns out?

Hey! This is supposed to be a positive time and here I go again spewing gloom and doom! Stop that, now, Craigy! (gentle, but firm slap to the hand)

Back to Sundays. I guess the lesson was that since we all have to take so much from others as we grow up, that it's only right and fair that we put something back whenever we can. I really do believe that a World of takers - or a town or neighborhood or even a family of takers - destroy one another as surely as death itself. Harley would say (and has, often!), "I don't owe nobody, nothin'!" I suppose that, technically, Harley is right. If parents have and raise their children just for the joy of helping to create and nurture a new human life and to get him ready to go out on his own and be successful in the World - then, kids don't owe them anything. The parents did all of that out of love - just because they wanted to - not ever expecting to be repaid. (Not all parents, of course, think that way - especially, I believe, the parents of the Harleys of the World.) (Sad, sad, face)

So, maybe, in the best of situations, we don't "owe nobody nothin'," but I still believe, 'owe' or not, it's just an appropriate part of being a member of society - of the human species, if you will - to put something back - whatever we can. Some can only do a little - others a lot. Some have time to give - others money - others service - others things - whatever - just something!

When I used to talk to Ginny about all the things I'd buy and all the places I'd go if I ever became rich, she'd just smile. She said I'd end up giving it all away anyway, so why even make such conjectures? Maybe she's right. I am a bit socialistic, I guess (and that seems to be a bad word in many quarters these days!). I do believe, though, that we should all share in the country's wealth. I'm not really sure how that should work. I'm in favor of free enterprise, also, and believe each person should be rewarded for his hard and/or diligent work. I'm against just plain old handouts - too proud myself for that - just like Mom and Pop. A mystery still, I guess, that someone else will just have to solve.

Now, Di, I've never had to go hungry or be cold, and I've never not had clean clothes in good repair to wear, so maybe I've not really been poor in the truest sense of the word. On the other hand, we've never had money enough for any frills like vacations, store-bought clothes (except occasionally), a car, shoes for everyday wear in the summertime, boots except for winter, ice cream cones, new furniture or an electric ice box - refrigerator.

Now, that has been poor, compared with most of the other families in and around Springfield. If we broke something, we fixed it, we couldn't just go out and get a new one. If we wanted or needed something we didn't have, we made it or scavenged or traded something for it. Somehow, Mom always found ways to keep wonderful new books in the house - well, not brand-new ones, you understand, but new to me. (I've always felt so sorry for kids who didn't treasure books.) (long, sad face)

Looking back, this was such a good kind of poor. You know, Di, we need at least two different words for poor. One for good poor (like in my life) and another for hurtful poor (like in Harley's life). - *Posipoor* and *Negapoor*! Daniel Webster, move over!

4:00 AM, July 5, 1952
20 hours left

Dear Diary,

I've been wondering, Di, why do you suppose I find it so easy to accept differences in most everybody else, but not in myself?

Mom and Pop have raised me to love, rather than to hate; to be involved, rather than to be unconcerned; to be intrigued, rather than to be put off by the new or the different. I've never heard either Mom or Pop put down anyone - really, Di, I haven't! That doesn't mean they give blanket approval to everything that goes on these days. Not by a long shot! They are, however, always careful to attack (for lack of a better word at the moment) the act or the idea or the movement, rather than the worth of the person or people involved. I can't always be that gracious yet at this age - usually, but not always. ("I don't dislike you, Ralph, but I really dislike how you treat people.")

At any rate, back to freaks (or didn't I mention yet that's the concept I'm pondering here?). When I encounter someone who somehow appears different from me or the rest of us, I'm drawn to them immediately. I want to learn about them. How did they become that way? What are the advantages and disadvantages of being that way? Why? How long have they been that way? How do they feel about being that way?

What effect has being that way had on their life, on their family and friends? So many questions immediately race through my mind! (Of course, I'd seldom, if ever, ask any of those questions to them at the outset. But I'd find ways of discovering the answers.)

If a difference in others had a bright side, I'd always try to find it - first for myself, and then to share it with them if they seemed bothered by it. Pollyanna? Sometimes, especially when younger and I truly couldn't see the larger picture. Not so much anymore, though.

I have to wonder why differences in others seem to be so scary to so many people. Not just scary, Di, threatening I believe is a more accurate term. Perhaps that's why for years we had the abominable 'Sundown Law' here in Springfield that made it unlawful for Negro people or Indians to stay in town past eleven at night. Disgusting. It has been gone several years now, but it irked me no end.

My old mountain man friend, Arnie, used to say that the better you get to know someone, the more the differences between you fade. In fact, he'd say, "When you really want to hate somebody, be certain you don't let yourself get to know them."

Take Arnie and me, as an example. To be perfectly honest, here, I was more than a little bit frightened by him the first time we met. I was eight. He was an unshaven, dirty, tobacco spitting, mule-team-driving, gargantuan specimen of humanity! I noticed that no one in town talked with him unless it was business. I wondered why. So, more than being frightened, I was cautiously intrigued. I'd follow him when he'd come to town (thinking, of course, he didn't know I was there!). I'd talk to his mules when he'd leave them alone for a time. They were so gentle! I listened to the men talk about him down at the feed store and at the cafe. I picked up many, many bits and pieces of information about Old Arnie.

One day, still with much trepidation, I admit, I walked up to him and announced in my squeaky little boy's voice, "I'm Craigy Franklin and I'd like to be your friend." (That was how Mom and Pop approached new folks at Church.) Do you know what Old Arnie did, Di? He took off his soiled old brown leather hat and extended his huge, ancient, greasy hand to me. The first time ever, a grown-up had offered to shake my hand! Boy, did I shake it! - far, far longer than necessary (or appropriate), but I wasn't about to let that big moment in my young life just pass!

We were instant friends, Arnie and me. So alike, and yet so different! Many of the townsfolk thought it was terrible that Mom and Pop let me be with him. I remember Mom's response on one occasion after Mrs. Mackey commented about that relationship to Mom: "My," Mom said, "I didn't realize that was any of your business, Mrs. Mackey!" (As close to "rude" as Mom ever became.)

Of course, Mom and Pop hadn't just let me go into that relationship without knowing it was safe. (They had both known Arnie for years.) I think Mom and Pop really got a kick out of seeing their pale, little, spit and polished, sandy-headed Craigy, sitting up there on that dilapidated wagon, beside what had to be the dirtiest, smelliest, biggest, blackest man in the county. Why, I've often wondered, could they be so amused and supportive, when most of the others in town were abhorred and disgusted? It was the differences, I think. The surface differences, really. They (the townsfolk) never let themselves get below the surface. Arnie was a kind and caring, gentle man – intelligent in his own ways, witty, and wise. But the townsfolk never got to know that. They missed out on so much just because they let those surface differences stand like a castle moat between them.

Di, if I were to have children, I'd do everything within my power to help them understand and appreciate that which is different. Akin to that, I think, is that Pop taught me to trust others until they showed me they couldn't be trusted. Along with that, I'd teach mine to seek out different sorts of folks and learn all they had to teach them. With all the coming changes in technologies and rapid transportation systems, our World is going to 'shrink', so to speak, so fast. We'll be exposed to so much that is different from that to which we have always been accustomed. If not us, then, our kids, at least, must be able to adapt, adopt, adjust and accept differences - benefit from them, in fact, the same way I have most certainly benefited from Arnie's differences.

We can't truly grow in knowledge and appreciation and

compassion, when we limit our experiences only to those which are familiar and similar to those we have known in the past. We only grow - we only stretch our minds and 'souls' to their finest limits, when we reach out to, and incorporate that which is different, unique, intriguing - even though, at first, it may seem frightening or even threatening. (Sermon number 1,000 by Craig Lee Franklin, Esq.!) We each must, of course, keep our own safety clearly in mind. (something between a smile and a sheepish grin)

I'm having trouble stickling to this freak thing, aren't I, Di? I've told you so often here in your pages, that I feel like a freak - too smart, too athletic, too popular, too orphan, too poor, too nice, too polite, too dependable, too romantically inexperienced, too small, too plain looking, and on and on and on - you know!

Well, those are all just differences - just uniquenesses. If they were attached to anybody else, I'd never ever think twice about them. It would be okay. It would be intriguing. But when they are attached to me, Di, I hate them! I detest them! I'd do anything to get rid of them! (Anything! I guess that's an appropriate and accurate term considering what day this is!) I can't in any way see them as wonderful. I only see them as terrible, despicable, unbearable millstones around my neck - choking away my life. Why is that, Di? I just hate myself for being like - or what - I am and the responsibilities they require. Mostly that – the responsibilities they require of me. I'm so unhappy, Di. I can accept almost anything, but not myself. Why doesn't someone help me, Di? People seem to forget that I am still just a kid in so many ways. Why won't anyone help me? I shouldn't even have to ask. (buckets of tears)

Terrible as this sounds, Di, I have often wished that it were the other way around - that I hated others and loved myself. That way, at least, I could get away from those I hated. But this way, I'm always here! The objects of my hate are all, always and forever, right here. (long, long, pause)

Well, I guess I really can't resolve that one. If I could, this whole exercise would be unnecessary, wouldn't it? Since, as William James might say, "Reality is what you think it is," I guess, in my view, I'll just die a freak.

It will soon be dawn. I want to be up at the cemetery when

dawn breaks this morning. I'll grab an orange (or three) and get going.

5:00 AM, July 5, 1952
19 hours left

Dear Diary,

Remember, Di, how as a little boy, I'd like to come up here to the cemetery and read the names and dates on the tombstones. I always felt this place was a link for me to the past - something I guess I felt I didn't really have anywhere else. I'd make up fantasies about all the people buried here. Decide who had known whom. Which ones liked one another? Which ones hadn't? How each one had died. Once, remember, I even set up a game of checkers between, P.J. VanWinkle and Elmer Jackson. I forget who won.

Remember how I used to stand right here and pretend I was talking to Mother and Father there in their graves. The townsfolk brought this tombstone for them, you know, Di. That was so nice. Someday I was going to get individual stones for each of them - guess not, now. I used to lay down in the grass between them – the space reserved for my grave – and look up at the sky to see what view I'd have.

I hope that now you understand, dear family, but as much as I have loved you in my fantasies, Mom and Pop Franklin are really my family. (pause to walk) I've made it clear I want to be buried down here beside Pop. Mom and I have talked about it (just in general, of course). She'll be on his right when her time comes, and I'll be on his left. We've been quite a team - Mom and Pop and Craigy!

Pop, there are so many things we never said to one another. I always knew you loved me, and I hope you knew how very much I loved you. We disagreed about a lot, didn't we! I guess that's the way it is between Pops and sons. I think you understood that all along. I didn't until just recently. I thank you for all the good times, and for the guidance and suggestions and corrections - even (I suppose) for the trips to the woodshed when I misbehaved. I don't think I'd spank my son, if I were to have one, but I know you meant well and you did make your points - got right to the seat of the problem, so to speak! (smiles for both of us)

I remember that day a few years ago when I got so mad at you - don't even remember what it was about now - just remember how determined I was to teach you a lesson. While you were reading the paper that evening, into the house I waltzed, adorned with a brand-new Mohawk haircut! I knew I had you now!! You looked up over your glasses, paused a moment and then said, in that calm, quiet voice of yours, "Well, I see you got a haircut. Thought it was about time," and went right back to reading the paper. The Mohawk was never spoken of between us. I suppose it ended up hurting Mom the most. She was so embarrassed. The townsfolk just couldn't believe that nice, well behaved, mild mannered, young pillar of the community, Craig Franklin, would ever do such a thing. Mohawks were for bad boys, everyone knew that!

It set the town a buzzing, but it never once seemed to ruffle your feathers, Pop. That day you taught me that revenge really couldn't be counted on to be sweet. You also taught me that no one could hurt you if you just refused to accept what they did or said as being hurtful to you. You were a wise man, Pop. How did you learn to be that way? I'm smart, but not yet wise. When does that come? How does one hurry the process? I've always been expected to be wise, just because I'm smart - to always make the right decisions - to do what was best and correct. How could people expect a little kid to have the wisdom that only seems to come with years and years of making and correcting and learning form one's own mistakes? Intelligent people are often so ignorant. I wonder why?

Remember, Pop, the time you caught me attempting to smoke my first (and last, by the way) cigar out behind the house! I wrote a verse for you about it. I was going to give it to you on your next birthday, but that birthday didn't have a chance to come for you. Well, Mom and I enjoyed it together at supper last night. We spent a lot of time remembering about you. It was a nice time. We both miss you so! Mom's doing okay, considering everything. You'd be proud of her, Pop. I am!

I found your private box up in the attic, Pop. I opened it. I hope you don't mind. You know, I never knew for sure what you thought about me writing verse and poetry and giving it to you for presents. You just never seemed to need or want anything. Pops are really hard to make gifts for. Sometimes I thought you might think I was a sissy for writing so much. When I found your box the other day, I realized that wasn't true. I didn't have any idea what I'd find inside. Just knew any box so carefully hand marked, "My Treasure Chest," must contain very precious things. Imagine my surprise and delight when I found it contained every poem I had ever written for you. See, Pop, even after you're gone, you're still answering big questions for me. Thanks Pop. Thanks for all ... Well, just thanks for choosing to be my Pop. I love you.

Over there, Di, is where Larry's buried. He was my best boyhood friend when I was little. We'd just turned six when he got appendicitis and died. He was the first child I had personally known who died. That was hard. One hour we were climbing the oak tree together and planning our tree house, and the next hour he was just dead. It wasn't fair. I cried and cried - more for me, I guess, than him. It was hard to lose such a good friend. I believed in heaven back then, and that was comforting. Larry had the best giggle in town. He loved to laugh. He'd listen to a joke, laugh his head off, and then say, "Tell it again," after which he'd do it all over!

After Larry died, life began getting much more serious and complicated. Now, I understand that it was the age, the time, the war - but back then, I thought it was because Larry had left me all alone. Sometimes I hated him so much for that - leaving me all alone!

Look over here, Di. See this little, flat, white limestone marker. It just says:

HANLEY
DIED - 1888

Even that is barely legible anymore - the stone is so weathered away. No one in town seems to know about him (or her?). I'd guess no one knew that person very well - there's no birth year, just the year he died. I wonder who he was, where he came from, how he died. Did people like him? Was he a good person? Why did he end up here - forgotten? I suppose in sixty years my marker will be just such a mystery. Suppose some little sandy-haired, six-year-old kid will find mine, and keep it cleaned up like I have for Hanley? It's nice to believe someone will do that someday - just because they want to - just because they think it's right - just because!

Down here, not too far from Pop, really, is where my dear, dear friend, Arnie Pascal lies. Mom and Pop and Ginny and Billy and John and Doc and Parson and I were the only ones at Old Arnie's funeral. I wrote a verse about him that says it all best, I think:

Ode to Arnie Paskal

Now, Arnie Pascal never thought
He'd be revered in rhyme,
And never knew how much he'd taught
Me, once upon a time.

Old Arnie never took a bath
And never read a verse.
He lived with mules, down the path -
I'm not sure which smelled worse!

On his mules I'd get to take
The greatest of all rides,
As we'd go fishing at the lake -
We'd eat the perch, fresh fried!

We'd fix his fence. His garden, rake.
Hitch mules up - just so.
What a pair we two would make
When into town we'd go!

He was a very patient man.
He'd let me try and try.

And always offered up a hand
To help this little guy.

We talked of dreams we both had had.
Of places I would go.
A wondrous friend for this young lad -
I loved Old Arnie so.

We only had about a year
And then my good friend died.
He told me not to shed a tear,
But I'm afraid I cried.

I knew that no one understood
What Arnie meant to me.
He taught me to be kind and good,
That caring was the key.

When I'm a Dad and sometimes lack
A sense of what to do,
I'll know, Good Friend, by looking back -
I *still* can count on you.

Rest in peace dear man, dear teacher, dear confidant, and dearest friend of all.

What name shall I have on my tombstone, Di? Shall it be the name Mother and Father, my biological parents gave me, or shall it be the one Mom and Pop gave me? I suppose the legal records would be less confused if it used my original name, after all, that is who I am supposed to be. But I know, deep inside, that at this point, I'm not that person. I'm Mom and Pop Franklin's son, through and through. I don't even know what it would mean to be that other person. Maybe in my next life (big, doubtful look), I'll return to being that person, but I want to die the way I've lived - a Franklin. ... I feel a poem forming ....

Who?

A little boy once had two names,
Then came the time he must
Decide which one he would remain
When he returned to dust.

There never really was a doubt -
A Franklin he had been.
The only life he'd known about.
Just Mom and Pop for kin.

Two words he wanted there upon
His tombstone be inscribed,
And so, into eternal dawn
'Twill ever read, "He Tried."

- Craig Franklin,
5:48 AM, 7/5/48

I am so tired, I am going to take just a little nap. I'll lie down here in the grass to the left of Pop - call it a practice run, I guess. (faint smile) Just a few minutes, then I'll get on with things.

6:00 AM, July 5, 1952
18 hours left

Dear Diary,
Halfway through these final 36 hours. Much yet left for me to do. This hour I'll just stay up here by Pop and write.
I know, I keep coming back to this, Di, but one of my biggest problems is the very thing everyone else seems to think is my very best asset. I can be - check that - I could have been, just about anything I wanted to be. I'm good at most things and I have always been interested in - no, downright fascinated by - everything! How in the World does one choose? What if I'd choose something I'd hate, or worse

yet, something at which I'd end up doing poorly?

The townsfolk all assume I'll become a physician because Doc and I have always been so close. I like science and helping people but being around sick people depresses me. I'd like the 'built in' respect that comes with being the town's doctor, but I'd really rather earn my respect all by myself - not have it built in. At the university, pre-med was a breeze. No problem there. But I don't enjoy it. Doc knows how I feel. He's all right about it. He understands.

I'd like to be so many things - an actor or a comedian. I really enjoy making people laugh and helping them forget about their cares for a little while. With humor, I can often help others see that their problems aren't really as big and bad as they thought they were.

I suppose I could use humor regardless of my profession. I think I'd like to be a psychologist or a psychiatrist. People's personal and emotional problems intrigue me, and I think I'm pretty good at helping people with those kinds of things. People have always said I am easy to talk with. My training in psychology would also help me in any field I might switch to later. So far, I have really enjoyed my studies in psychology. Psych profs are generally pretty good eggs - not at all like the stuffy, bearded, esoteric, Dr. Freud.

If, later, I'd become a writer (probably my first love, really), I know the psychology training would help me understand what makes people tick, so I could write more realistically - real motivation - you know what I mean, Di. I do love to write so - even this formless prattle I'm doing now. I really can write well, too, when I set my mind to it. When I take the time. I'm afraid this diary (no offense, Di) won't win any awards for grammar or structural precision. But, that's not my purpose here. From mind to paper without ever being refined or censored in any way. True, honest, real, open, gut level, heart level thoughts. I don't have to be precise, exact, picky or correct. I can just relax and let it flow. That's really nice, Di. It's one reason you've always helped me think so clearly. Nobody to please but you and me - and you never complain! What a team, Di. (smile) When I read through my entries, it often seems as though you really are a friend, Di - I mean like you are a living, breathing, thinking friend.

I'd also like to be an inventor. I've always loved making things that have never been made before - Remember the five wheeled unicycle I built. No one ever fell of that baby, I'll tell you! My record storage cabinet that remembers where each record is and pushes it out for me when I punch the right buttons. The metal, tubular stilts that can adjust up and down pneumatically. The toothbrush with the built-in paste dispenser in the handle. The automatic door closer I invented for Mr. Elzer at the grocery. The pickle barrel that automatically raises its bottom up as pickles are removed from the top, so you don't have to ever dig very deep to get the ones you want. Remember when I tied bells on Perry's shoes so his mother could keep track of where he was. The new set of chisels I designed for my wood sculpturing.

In my deepest, darkest fantasies, I sometimes see myself working in a ritzy hotel, catering to very rich young lady guests. I keep them company and attend to all their needs for a fee - a gigolo, I believe is the high-class term. I'd never do it for real, but it makes wonderful fantasies!

I could be a professional musician - piano, clarinet, trombone, saxophone. I'd really like to play the marimba or vibes. Wouldn't it be great to have a trio of muffled trap drums, a lower register clarinet and vibes! Now that would have a great, mellow sound! We could travel and see the whole country, meet beautiful women and maybe even become famous. I'm afraid my mind would go stale doing that - same thing, day in and day out. I go nuts if I miss a day of not putting my mind through its paces.

When I was younger, I was sure I'd be a carpenter. I really do love to build. I built Mom new kitchen cabinets when I was just thirteen. They really are beautiful (if I do say so, myself!), with inlaid wood patterns on the doors, and butcher-block type counter tops. They are lighted inside. She really loves them. Pop was so proud of me.

Even before that - I guess at about nine - I remodeled half of our attic into my own private room. Remember when I decided to make insulation from shredded newspapers treated so they were fire resistant. Nobody around here ever heard of 'insulating' a house. I did the whole place before I was done. We hardly have to heat the place in winter and in summer it stays cool till mid-afternoon. The townsfolk still think I'm a bit crazy for doing that - let them! It's amazing what you can learn how to do from books. If they'd only read! Someday every building constructed will be insulated, you mark my word!

I've been fixing and re-fixing my room ever since. The fire pole outside my window for rapid starts (or emergency get-a-ways). My favorite is the periscope I fixed to use as a light source at my desk. Just turn it ever so slightly every half hour or so (keeping it pointed at the sun) and it floods my desktop with soft, wonderful light. Moonshine doesn't work so well!

I suppose I could have been an artist - I'd probably opt for sculpture - I really enjoy sculpting. I already have one piece in the rotunda at the state capital (or is it capitol - can never keep those two straight). It's my pioneer piece - pioneers, covered wagon, horses, complete with little brother teasing his sister. I could enjoy doing that. Probably most pieces would have some humorous or ironic twist to them. I can work on a piece all day and night and totally lose track of time. That reminds me that I still have to finish my gift for Mom for next Christmas. Later.

My teachers always thought I'd end up being a philosopher - me always quoting Socrates, Aristotle, James and Descartes. I love to play with ideas - right vs. wrong - perfection vs. imperfection - what is real vs. what is illusion. I'm not sure that accomplishes much beyond just the fun of it. Your great ideas get stored in dusty old books where mankind basically ignores them and just goes on being its selfish, war-waging, bigoted self. (My, aren't we the pessimistic one, here, Craig!) If I truly thought I could save the World, I'd stick around. That was always one of my goals. Save mankind from itself.

Coach says, I have to continue swimming. He says I have World Class potential (whatever that is), but to do that, you just have to totally immerse yourself (no pun intended) in that one sport - train eight to ten hours a day, 365 days a year. That would just limit my life too much - look who's talking about limiting one's life, Di. Strikes me quite humorously just now. Laughed out loud, in fact! But, anyway, I'd rather swim for the fun of it. When I moved up to pool swimming, I never got comfortable being forced to wear a suit!

I always thought I'd like to be a teacher - help little kids discover how wonderful - wonder-filled - it is to learn new things. If I didn't learn something new every day, I doubt if I could get to sleep at night. Really! I owe that to Pop. At night, before I'd go off to bed, he'd always ask me what I knew that day, that I hadn't known the day before. Long after he stopped asking, I'd still stop by his room at night and tell him about what ever new and wonderful things I'd discovered or thought about that day. After I was eleven or so, I know he really didn't understand much of what I was telling him, but he did understand my enthusiasm and my determination to keep searching for new ideas and new truths. I think he was very pleased he had done that to me. I am, too!

If a teacher would just concentrate on doing that to the students, he wouldn't have to teach a thing - the students would become non-stop, self-motivated learning machines - like I have been, I guess. I'm sure that you have to begin instilling that really early in life, though - way before first grade. Perhaps I'd have ended up as a teacher of really young children. In Germany (excuse my language) they call it Kindergarten - at least one excellent idea that came out of Germany this century. What a wonderful name - Kinder (child) garden, as if you just plant them there, nurture them, and watch them utilize their own resources and those you provide, as they grow and prosper!

In many ways, I'd like to just be an Arnie Paskal. I could survive all on my own - I could teach little kids one at a time. I could sculpt when I felt like sculpting, write when I was so moved, think great thoughts each evening while contemplating the stars, fill my home with wondrous gadgets and inventions. I could walk and run and swim - play my marimba, perhaps even build my own house from scratch (well, *wood* might work better!). Perhaps, I'd even entertain beautiful ladies several nights a week!!! (Unlike Arnie, you see, I *would* bathe!)

You know, Di, that really is the life I'd like to live, but it doesn't use any of these damn gifts of mine, for the benefit of anybody but me. That's selfish and I couldn't do that. What about that! I can't be what I want to be, because I'm somebody who has to be something else! I guess I know how

Princess Elizabeth must feel. She could never become a teacher or a nurse, because she has to grow up to be Queen. Elizabeth, you have my deepest sympathies!!!

7:00 am. July 5, 1952
17 hours left

Dear Diary,
    In seventeen hours, I'll no longer be a living organism, Di. Gone forever and I know it. I think it is wonderful. You probably think it is morbid. I don't mean it's wonderful that I'm about to kill a seventeen-year-old genius. That is truly terrible. I am totally ashamed of that.
    What is wonderful to me, though, Di, is knowing *when* I will die. It's given me time to prepare. Time to put things in order. That's what I meant by wonderful. I've always felt bad for families left behind when someone just dies unexpectedly with no warning - like in a car accident or from a heart attack - you know. They didn't have time to put things in order - to say their good-byes - to be able to soften the blow for their loved ones - to say those things you have always wanted or needed to say but didn't.
    I never, ever wanted to go that way. I knew that even long before I decided to end my life this way. Pop knew he was going, I am sure. He just became weaker and weaker. I'm sure he knew. But, that way he had time to say good-bye. To put things in order. To let us show him our love, through those, last, difficult days and nights. He hurt so much those last weeks. I'm glad his hurting could stop. It won't be long now, Di, until my hurting can also stop. Mom's hurting, I guess, will begin all over again. (?)
    I'm just going to walk and think for a little while, now.

8:00 AM, July 5, 1952
16 hours left.

Dear Diary,

When I was fifteen - about this time last year, I guess, - I wrote a poem about my favorite climbing tree. I'm sitting up here in it, now, Di - out behind the house. It's always been one of my safe places. I think that poem may tell more about me than I could have imagined when I was writing it. It just flowed off the pen. Hardly a correction or revision - a lot like the way, "WHO" emerged a few hours ago. They both just wrote themselves - sometimes poems do that, Di. Somehow, they are always the best ones - I mean really revealing - personally meaningful - as if there is a spot deep inside my mind with nothing to do but devise verses and then, just wait for the opportune moment to spring them on me. Those are also the easy ones to remember.

My Thinking Tree

I guess that most young kids have had
A tree or two to climb.
But one was special for this lad -
The place, the age, the time.

It stood alone beside our fence.
Rose up to such a height!
It was my very best defense
From bullies, work and fright.

The more I had upon my mind
The higher up I'd go,
In hope some answers I could find
Up there, where breezes blow.

There was one very special crotch
That made me feel content -
'Bout halfway up, where I could watch
The neighborhood events.

To be down lower wasn't fun,

'Cause then I wouldn't know
What kind of things were being done
Throughout the yards below.

And any higher let me see
Just way too far away.
It made me question how'd life be,
Beyond my realm of play.

I sometimes drift my mind there yet
When feeling not so wise,
And after a while, the biggest threat,
Gets cut right down to size.

I guess I'll just sit up here a while, quietly, Di, and see if my thinking tree can work its magic one final time.

9:00 AM, July 5, 1952
15 hours left

Dear Diary,
No magic from my tree, today. I guess I've used it all up. I'm on my way back up to my room - that explains the more jiggley, than usual, handwriting, here, Di. I just have a few finishing touches to put on Mom's Christmas present. I had to start quite early this year. It's a clay sculpture. I call it Faces Of Craig. It's a bust of me about eighteen inches high, but instead of one full, three-dimensional head, it's a composite of four faces, one on each side - my face at four different ages.

The earliest photo I could find of me, was taken when I was about four, so that is face number one - uncombed hair with shaggy bangs down over my eyebrows, a smudge on my cheek, firmly set jaw (obviously saying, "Don't bother me for a photograph now, when I'm in the middle of ... whatever!").

The second, is at about ten. It's the first school picture we could afford to buy. I was a freshman, so of course, I wore a tie. My hair was slicked back and shiny. My patented grin was in place. Eyes wide. (Terrified, perhaps.) I still had those rounded little boy features and turned up nose.

The third, was at thirteen. It's from a newspaper article about the governor selecting my *Westward Ho!* sculpture to be on permanent display at the capitol. A thinner face than before, sadder eyes, I think - to be quite truthful, it's a pretty homely kid! (smile)

The final face is from a picture I had Ginny take about a month ago. It's my all-time favorite picture of me - I suppose because it flatters me a bit (heck, a lot!). Just a hint of a smile this time. A bit more tired looking. Older. It would qualify, I think, as the portrait of a man.

The bust won't be dry enough to wrap, but I have a big red bow to drape over it, and a special card I made for her. Next hour I'll write my final poem - a Christmas poem to put in her card. I must get to work now, Di. Having trouble with those sleepy eyes. Please excuse me.

10:00 AM, July 5, 1952
14 hours left

Dear Diary,

It really looks great - the sculpture. Except for the one in the museum, maybe, it's the best piece I've ever done. I'm really proud of it! Faces are difficult for me to sculpt. My own seemed even harder. Mom always had a thing about liking to touch my face. I think when Mom touches those faces, she'll be able to feel close to me. I've left information about having it fired.

Now for the poem. I'm up on the hill behind the school playing field. No one will interrupt me here, and the pine trees remind me of Christmas. It's hard to be inspired to write about Christmas when it's already 85 degrees plus in the shade. No problem - I've been forming this one in my mind all week. It's another one of those that should pretty well just flow from wherever they form. I'll try it out on you here first, Di, then copy it onto the card later.

The Very Best Christmas Tree

At Christmas time the big event

Was trimming our fine tree!
Would stand so tall. Have fresh pine scent.
The finest it could be!

We made our ornaments by hand
From cloth and yarn and wood.
Each one, so carefully, we planned -
Turned out just as they should!

Now just before the star was set,
With popcorn garlands strung,
A cup of cocoa we'd all get,
While carols there were sung,

Pop placed the star atop our tree -
One Grandmother had fixed.
She hand-crocheted it, carefully,
Way back in ought and six.

Each year, Mom thought, that tree, the best
That she had ever seen.
Somehow it stood out from the rest -
So tall and bright and green!

Mom, looking back, you're right, you know!
Each year was truly best,
But 'twasn't tree or bells or snow -
'Twas family love, confessed!

Merry Christmas, Mom
Craigy, 1952

I really like that one, Di. It made me cry as I wrote it. Sorry, I got you all wet. It was a good cry. Perhaps my last really good cry.

Next hour is going to be so tough - I'm meeting Ginny for lunch. Oh, how I hope I can keep myself collected. My mouth is already dry. Order lots of Grapette, Craig! Lots and lots of Grapette! This is going to be so tough!

11:00 AM, July 5, 1952
12:00 Noon, July 5, 1952

12 hours to live

Dear Diary,

My time with Ginny took the whole hour, so I'll write about it here. She really wanted to do the talking today. I mostly just listened. She's so bright - so insightful - so sensitive. She's going to make a great mother someday. I hope she has a whole passel of kids - like the Old Lady in the Shoe, only Ginny *will* know what to do!

It was like every talk we'd ever had. Comfortable, reassuring. I got so involved, like usual, that I forgot for a few minutes it was being our last talk. She's so excited about her senior year. She'll be first chair alto sax and will work on the Yearbook staff. She's taking advanced composition and biology - two subjects she really loves. Geometry, she's not looking forward to. She said I'd have to be prepared to tutor her, nightly, in that. I smiled and nodded. That's when I came back into focus - this was it! Had she not been so bubbly and excited, she'd have caught my reservations about future commitments. I'm glad she didn't!

Sunday, she and Mark are playing a piano-saxophone duet at church. They do everything so well together. She's going to his place after church for dinner. That's nice. (Mark's mother makes the best fried chicken in the county! Please don't tell Mom I said that.)

At one point, quite off the subject, I asked her, "Do you think I'm a freak?" At first, she laughed and didn't take me seriously, but when my own expression didn't change, she sobered up and asked, "Whatever do you mean, Craigy? A freak! How a freak?"

I rambled on a while and she listened. She's a great listener - like you, Di. Ginny says everybody our age feels like freaks, sometimes - her too. That's hard to believe! She insisted that 'different' didn't mean 'freak'. She said I was unique, intriguing, unusual and fascinating, but not a freak. Hear that, Di. I'm unique, intriguing, unusual and fascinating! Why do I still feel like a freak?

She said I seemed a little down - but a lot less than I had been, recently. (I told you she was insightful, Di!) I turned *up* the smile and, on the charm, and convinced her I was just tired. I think I wanted her to pursue that, but she didn't. At that, I felt both relieved and desperately cheated! I don't know why for sure. I suppose it's because she'd never, ever, let me hide anything from her before, and I was expecting one of her friendly inquisitions. I guess that's okay. No! It really isn't okay! I want so much to explain to her what I'm about to do. I want her, of all people, to know and understand my reasons. I want her respect, and if I should lose it over this, I'll have no way to ever convince her otherwise.

I'll have to go with that as it is. I certainly couldn't ever tell her and let her feel guilty. You know, Di, it's really hard to say "Good-bye" to someone, when that person doesn't know what you're trying to say. (long sigh, sober face)

1:00 PM, July 5, 1952
11 hours to live

Dear Diary,

Just got my haircut at Jimmy's Barber Shop. I'm so vain, Di, I can't let myself die without getting a haircut, so I'll look neat when I'm laid out! I really never thought of myself as being vain, until these past few days. I find myself looking at my reflection most everywhere it appears - puddles, store windows, and mirrors, of course. It's weird. It's like I'm looking at me, but it isn't really me doing the looking. Strange!

I wonder how many times old Jimmy has cut my hair. Mom always used to cut it when I was small. We couldn't afford the store-bought variety. Then, Jimmy started giving out a free one for every A+ we boys got on our report cards. He still has plenty of hash marks on the wall for me to use up. Looks like I get free cuts till I'm forty!

I have wondered if he started all this just so I could get the kind of haircuts all the other boys got. I wouldn't put it past him. I told him today, I felt as though I was taking advantage of his good intentions, and I offered to begin paying. He said, "One last trim, then, on Old Jimmy." And so it was - one last trim!

Have to run. I can just make my date with Parson. Hope he's in top form today! (smile, I guess?)

2:00 PM, July 5, 1952
10 hours to live

Dear Diary,

I just came from Parson's study. I like and respect him a great deal as a person and friend, but our beliefs about religious questions have certainly grown apart since I was younger. Of course, when I was younger, my beliefs were Parson's beliefs, weren't they!

When I was small, I went to Church and Sunday school every Sunday without fail. I learned about the Church and God, the Trinity, Heaven and Hell. I said my prayers each night. Then, as I grew older, I studied the Christian scriptures there. I was even baptized like a good boy should be. Understand, Di, I'm not sorry for any of that.

Remember the furor I caused when, on that Youth Sunday, I preached from the Koran rather than from the Bible! I was somewhat amazed and amused that the truly good people of that church seemed to purposely keep themselves so ignorant about what the other great religions of the world taught and believed. They didn't want to know - no, more than that, they were offended, even seemed scared, to hear about differing beliefs. Willful, intentional, ignorance – that in and of itself should be a sin! (And not one thing I read there, was in any way different from the very same idea from the Bible. If it weren't the difference in ideas they objected to, then what was it – the *book* those same ideas came from? Abject ignorance!)

When those other beliefs were mentioned, it was usually only to point out why they were wrong, rather than to see what they might have to offer - to teach us. It's like no one except Christians have ever had a good, pure, meaningful thought about religion or living the good life. It's scary, but they really DO believe that religious ignorance is bliss.

They particularity didn't like the part where I suggested that people who lived a good life for the primary purpose of getting themselves into heaven, were really very selfish folks. That a good life should be lived for the purpose of helping to improve the human condition - better the lot of our fellow men - to advance useful knowledge. That the focus of our lives should be on helping others in the here and now, rather than on our own reward in the hereafter. Needless to say, Di, Parson really squirmed throughout my presentation. (I really enjoyed that! Aren't I terrible!)

Luckily, I think - as I look back on it - I left out the part where I logically showed the fallacy of the god-concept. You've heard of being stoned to death - I fear I would have been *hymnalled* to death on the spot! (smile, impish smile)

I talked about the same subjects with Parson again today. I think I really hoped he'd have found some way to convince me of God's existence. He tried! Still didn't make sense. It's all based on faith and Parson concluded today that I just don't seem to have any! (So fortunate are those who do!)

I told him I had all kinds of faith - faith in myself, faith in good people, faith in the potential for most people to be good, faith in the scientific process of discovery, faith in the lessons of history, faith in the creative processes - I went on and on and on, Di. He said that was all fine and dandy, but that without God, all of that was meaningless. I contended the opposite - no need to have faith in any of the things on my list, if you had faith in god, because god was the reason for, and the answer to all things.

Parson kept coming back to, "But how do you explain this Universe unless God created it?" And I countered, "How do you explain how god, himself was created?" He'd say, "God has always been, so we don't need to explain His creation." I'd say, "I would rather stop at the point of just saying that the universe (or its components) has always been - to pile on a creator-concept just moves it all one step further than seems necessary. If god could have always been, then why couldn't the universe just always have been, instead?"

It's like the old-time round of explanations about how the

Earth stays in place in the sky. First, Atlas held it on his shoulders. That was fine for a time, but then, a large turtle had to be concocted for Atlas to be standing on, and then, later still, a sea was added for the turtle to be swimming in and on and on and on. I say stop with explanations at the first possible step. Of course, I can't fathom how a universe (or anything else) could have always been. 'Always' just isn't possible to understand with the human brain - at least not with mine. But why mess it up with even more unexplainables?

Okay, I understand more folks are on Parson's side than on mine and that Parson and I will never agree, but he's always been such a good sport through these discussions. He's so patient with me. Even if I believe his motivation for being a good guy is misplaced - to get himself into heaven - he is a superior human being and I love him deeply.

I guess I shouldn't fault the church for using the fear of hell to control its members into being nice people. When it works, it helps, doesn't it! I really do get angry inside, though, when people use their own brand of religious belief to harm or terrorize or destroy or badger others who hold differing beliefs. Witch hunts! The Christian Crusades! Ku Klux Klan! Hate the Jews movements! Hate the Negro movements! Well, you get the idea, Di. I thought religion was about loving, but, so often it seems to be about hating or at least about excluding.

Here in our good town, Di (and I mean good in a most sincere, not sarcastic, way), our Christian townsfolk had, for years, a law on the books that made it illegal for a Negro or American Indian to stay in town overnight. The town fathers were so proud (really, they were – I was here!) that we had no racial problems here in Springfield. Negroes could work here and shop here and worship here - so long as it's done prior to the Six P.M. curfew - but they may not live here.

Even Parson agrees with me that it was a terrible law, but as a boy I couldn't convince him to attack it. He said he'd lose his effectiveness as a minister to his flock, if he publicly took a position which would be so unpopular with them. I called him two-faced. He agreed that, indeed, he was, and added that he hoped when the passions of my youth mellowed, I would understand. Who knows? I am thankful that I will be leaving behind a community that ridded itself of that despicable law.

It sounded like Parson was equating the waning of passion with the development of wisdom. I wonder? I know I'm not wise yet - guess I never will experience wisdom, since it only seems to come with living long, and learning well, the lessons one observes.

Arnie Pascal was wise. I always wondered if that was because he had no formal education to get in the way of wisdom and to delay it's emerging? Virtually everything that he knew, he taught himself – he'd say, nature taught him. Arnie was such a contented person. So at peace with himself and his universe. So understanding and non-condemning of others - even of the townsfolk who made such fun of him. I've tried to figure out what Arnie would say to me now, if he knew about my desperate thoughts. I do know, of course! He'd say, "Be your own man, live your own life, mend your own fences, and help your neighbors mend theirs. You may be able to help save your own little corner of the World, but don't take on the whole World by yourself," or words to that effect.

Oh, how I wish I could be that way, Di. But too many people have done too much for me, and most of them expect repayment from me by making myself into something great and wonderful. How do you let such caring, generous people down, and then face them? I don't think I could, so, shortly now, I'll just let them all down, once and for all, in the biggest, most terrible way possible - one that selfishly assures me, I won't have to face them afterwards. Coward? Certainly! Despicable? Undoubtedly! Still, the only answer for me? I truly believe so! ...

Hey, let's not end this entry on such a sour note. Parson said something to me this afternoon that won't slip into the back of my mind. I'm not sure if it's comforting or distressing? It just sits there, right behind my forehead - big and bold, and more than a little unnerving. I remember his exact words: "It may be somewhat inappropriate for me to say this to you, Craig, but you know, you are the finest Christian boy I have ever known, who does not believe in God, Christ or the Holy Spirit!" We chuckled! Then we laughed out loud! He meant it - his eyes told me that! Just what was it that he meant? ... Well, I'm going to take it as a complement and leave it at that.

3:00 PM, July 5, 1952
9 hours to live

Dear Diary,
[Alert: some will consider this a vulgar passage.]

There once was a beauty named Sharon.
Best liked, when no clothes, she was wearin'.
She'd bed any boy!
Was every guy's toy!
Her baby, twelve guys, must now share in!

I wrote that awful limerick during a "Truth or Dare" game one night when I was camping out with the guys. Either tell them about the first time I'd had sex with a girl (fat chance for the truth, there!), or be dared to write a dirty verse for them about Sharon. I think they realized I had no choice! Craigy, the goody-goody, had obviously never done the big IT! Thus, the limerick! Took all of five minutes to write.

Not that it didn't tell the truth about Sharon - it did, indeed! But I felt bad afterwards, anyway - I felt kind of dirty all over. The verse eventually made its way to the wall of the boy's rest room at the High School. Luckily, I had already moved on from there, or Mr. Kelley would have had my hide! Poor Sharon. She's had two babies already, and she's just my age. She may be pregnant again, I hear. Surely, no girl can really be that stupid.

Should I go find her like I had planned or shouldn't I, Di?

I guess I can at least go by her place and see if she's there. That sounds reasonable. More later.

Later. ... Well, I saw her. We talked. For some dumb reason I ended up telling her I had written that limerick, and I apologized. She thanked me - not for the apology, mind you, oh no! For the limerick! - She thought it was "so cute." Where is her head?

One thing seemed to be leading to another and I got up and left!

4:00 PM, July 5, 1952
8 hours to live

Dear Diary,
    I just ran out to Bennett's Cliff and back. The physical exertion felt good.
    On the way back, I stopped at the dentist's office and made an appointment for tomorrow morning at 10:00. I know, Di, I won't be around to keep it, but when I don't show up (very, very unlike good old punctual, dependable Craig Franklin), Dr. Funk will call Mom, and Mom will call Billy. He'll call Ginny and soon they'll all be looking for me. Since Ginny knows I'm planning to camp out tonight by myself under the trestle by the swimming hole, they'll find me in no time.
    Why is that so important, Di? Vanity, again, I guess. I don't want to just lay out there and rot, you know! Also, the little guys go swimming there late afternoons this summer, and I sure don't want them to have to find me - that would be terrible for them - a terrible thing for me to have done to them.
    Eight hours to live - give or take a half hour or so. Funny, an eight-hour workday usually seems so long - an eight-hour life, suddenly seems so short. Misgivings yet? None! I think that once I made the final decision yesterday, nothing could probably stop me now, anyway. (Not a very scientific approach to the biggest deal in your entire life, Craig!)
    I know I could feel sad for Mom and Ginny and my other friends if I'd let myself. I'm sure I could also give myself a huge case of the guilts if I'd allow it - but I won't. So, upward and onward as they say. (I've always wondered who *they* were, Di. Any ideas?)

5:00 PM, July 5, 1952
7 hours to live

Dear Diary,
    We're at the gravel pit below Bennett's Cliff - Just you and me, Di. I brought some hot dogs to roast and some potato chips to munch on, an apple, and four - count them - four

packages of Twinkies - I love Twinkies! Some folks would say that's not much of a last meal, I guess, but it's just exactly what I want. I have a little fire going - letting it burn way down to red hot coals - that roasts the best hot dogs. I've cut a stick from a maple tree - long and strong and just green enough so some of its sweet sap will seep into the hot dogs as they roast!

Mr. Elzer threw in the apple when I told him I was camping out tonight. He's sure has been good to me over the years, there at the grocery store. Five years I've worked part time for him. We used to talk about fixing up the room upstairs in back for me to live in when I left home. He'd have done it for me, too. Mr. Elzer is a fine man!

Even with my shirt off, it's still hot at five p.m., Di. There's a little breeze, though - probably more up on the cliff. I'll hike up there after I eat. The water looks so smooth. The sun gives it an orange tint across the way, and then it just gradually fades to gray up close here. Probably prettier than a gravel pit deserves to be. It's so deep that the water is always way to cold to be any fun for swimming. It's pretty good fishing - at least that's what John tells me. I'm not much into fishing since Arnie passed on.

... The sun doesn't even seem to be falling. Like it doesn't want to set - holding onto daytime for as long as it can. I guess that's fine with me, today.

... Gee, it's beautiful and peaceful out here. I've always loved to be alone here at dusk. The sky, the trees, the lengthening shadows, the swallows and bats, the flowers and the grass. Even the stones and pebbles seem especially pretty today. As a little boy I became fascinated by how as the light faded away, the colors in the flowers also faded away.

...I'm now eating the best hot dog ever made, Di. I brought four along, but I think this one is going to be all I'll want. Not real hungry.

...Eating more for memories than anything else, I guess.

...Did you ever notice the sound an apple makes when you first bite into it? Sort of like when you stab a bank of frozen snow with a shovel, or when you toss a scoop of popcorn into the skillet for popping - like when you open a bottle of Grapette. Wish I had some, I'm thirsty. Guess a drink out of the pit won't kill me! (smile)

...Four packages of Twinkies, all in a row - and just for me. I'm sure I've never done that before! My, were they ever good! The first did seem better than the last, though. Interesting!

...Just went wading. Boy is it cold! The ledge here is only about six feet wide so you really have to be careful or you'll be into forty feet of water in a hurry. It's a wonder no kid has ever drowned out here. I suppose the cold water temperature has helped keep kids away.

...An ant had just made his way to the top of my roasting stick (I had it stuck in the sand). He seemed so surprised when he got up there that there was no place else to go. I understand, little ant. ... So, I put him down here beside me on a potato chip. Thought I'd share! (smile) That couldn't have been more than five minutes ago. Now there must be a hundred of his little pals there with him trying their darndest to carry off that chip - Good luck little buckaroos.

I've always wondered where ants keep themselves - in ant hills, I know, Di - but I mean, there won't be an ant anywhere in sight, and five minutes after you drop a crumb on the ground, there they are. It happens no matter where you are. Even up in our attic! How do they know? Do you realize, Di, how many ants that means there must be in this world! Ants must make up a significant portion of the weight of this planet! (furrowed forehead) Several times I've tried to write a poem about the lowly, but ubiquitous ant. It just never seemed to develop. Guess the ant's praises will just have to be sung by some other bard.

...Guess, I'll put out the fire and hike up to the cliff. There's something I've always wanted (needed?) to do up there. Let's see if old Craigy F. can muster the guts to do it!

6:00 PM, July 5, 1952
6 hours to live

Dear Diary

Here we are, Di, sitting up on Bennett's Cliff overlooking the gravel pit. We've been here often - you and me. They say the water in the pit is 60 feet deep directly below me. That's deep! That's a lot of water.

When I was younger, Pop asked me not to swim in the pit because he thought it was too dangerous. I've only disobeyed that request a couple of times - only when I was dared. Dumb, but true! If it is dangerous when you're not being dared, then it certainly is still dangerous when you are being dared. Dumb teen macho mentality.

I always wished I had the courage to dive off from up here. It's about 40 feet down to the water. Looks a lot higher from up here than from down below - I jumped off, feet first, once last summer. That was bad enough! I want to dive though - headfirst. I really need to do that! ... after while, I guess. We'll see.

There are a lot of things I wish I would have done, Di. Some things, like diving off Bennett's Cliff that I was too scared to do. Other things I just didn't make time for. Some things, of course, I didn't have the chance to do.

I've never flown an airplane, Di. I really would like to do that - just never had the chance. I've never been snow skiing, either. I think I'd really like that - the speed - the danger - the thrill! This may sound dumb, but I really would have liked to travel in a submarine. I think I'd like to study the oceans - maybe be on the first submarine to travel around the World underwater - Captain Craig Nemo - that's me!

I've written a lot of things, Di - stories, poems, plays, even a musical - but never anything really great. I wish I'd have taken the time to create some really great literary work. Something that would change the world (or at least some of the people in it) for the better. I've written a poem every day since I was seven. How many did I figure that was - almost four thousand! Can you imagine that! Just one little thing that takes about twenty minutes a day, added to tomorrow and the next day, and before you know it, four thousand! Boy, if I could sell those suckers for a buck each, I'd be rich!

Life's like that, Di. It's the little things that really add up in the long run. People must not forget the little things. You know (of course you don't know, but pretend, Di. Just pretend!) You know how great you feel when someone - a perfect stranger - just smiles at you or waves at you or says,

"Hi. How's it going!" I mean, that really is the best feeling to me. They don't even know me, and yet they are willing to take the time and make the effort to recognize me and to say, "Hey, Kid, you're important to me just because you're a person out there." I think everyone must get a rush of happy security inside them when that happens. I wonder? I wonder if other people even think about it? They should. It is like the glue that holds our society together – dependable decency between people.

That's one of the ways I came to learn that the World was a safe and caring and helpful place. I wish I'd have done that more often for others. I wonder how many folks I've just passed on sidewalks in my lifetime who really needed that kind of reassurance - just a smile, a kind word - and I failed to deliver it because I was too busy or self-absorbed? Too busy doing what? I could have helped, but I didn't! How much extra time could it take - none, probably, since I'd already have been there - the time was already spent. All I needed to do was fill that time with a smile and a friendly word instead of filling it with indifference. Yes, I wish I'd have tried harder to show others that their world, or at least my corner of it, was a good and caring and safe place for them.

I wish, as a boy, I'd have taken on the town fathers about the Sundown Law. That was so unfair - so wrong - so loathsome! One set of human beings dictating to another set, what they can and can't do - where they can and can't be. It's like slavery really never ended. I wish I'd tried harder to do something about that. I have the feeling Mom and Pop expected me to do that. Well, in the end I did help, but Pop never knew.

I wish I could have been a father - I think I'd have been a good one - I've had so many good fatherly models in my life - Pop, of course, was the greatest (though I didn't always think so at every moment in my life!). Arnie was so special! I'd probably try to be a lot like him if I were to become a father - patient, caring, but not overprotective, easy going, yet demanding. Parson - integrity, that's what he's all about (except for the Sundown Law thing!) and living by a set of well-constructed and well thought through values - knowing what you believe and making those beliefs obvious to others at all times. And Doc. What can I say? I respect him so very much. Seems I only went to him when I was in (or thought I was about to be in) big trouble.

I'd have been sure my kids knew what I believed and why, but I would have wanted and encouraged them to look at a whole lot of other sets of beliefs so they could choose the ones that made the most sense to them. After all, Mom and Pop's values worked well for them, but today, you have to change them a bit to fit new knowledge, new opportunities, new lessons from history. Mine, undoubtedly, wouldn't work as they are for my children in their world, either.

I do wish I were going to see this world fifty years from now. It will be an exciting period - from horses to jet cars - from water power to atomic and solar power - from a world divided into little, self-interested countries, to a united world, working together for the common good of all mankind - from just looking at the moon and Mars through telescopes, to actually exploring them in person with rocket ships - from black and white and yellow and red thinking, to thinking like one Family of Man all over the World. It is to be a wonderful period in man's history that I will be missing, Di.

Well, my hour is up. A lot of those things I wish I had done, or wish I could do someday, I just won't be able to do, but I can dive off Bennett's Cliff headfirst! I'll tell you how it went next hour, Di. ... Boy is this theee scariest thing I've ever done or what! ... You guard my pile of clothes, Di. ...

H E R E   G O E S!...

7:00 PM, July 5, 1952
4 hours to live

Dear Diary,
WOW, Di! WOW! I did it! Straight as an arrow - I screamed at the top of my lungs all the way down, but I did it! WOW! Craig Franklin dived off Bennett's Cliff. WOW! Unfortunately, Craig Franklin is also the only one who will ever know about it, but I guess that's all that really matters anyway. WOW! I have to calm down. I'll get dressed and calm down.

... Okay. Well, the time is drawing near now, and still a lot left to accomplish. If I'd have been this well-organized all my life, just think how much I could have accomplished. I'm sitting here up against the Big Oak - I suppose that's capitalized - it's always just been called, Big Oak. Anyway, I'm sitting here like so many times before. It's the tree I carved my name in last year on my 16th birthday. Under my name, I just now carved the years of my life - 1931 - 1952. Seems pretty final, now, Di. Pretty final.

Not much of a legacy, I guess - 26 letters carved into an old, and very mortal, tree. I wonder how long the tree will live yet. Arnie guessed it was at least fifty years old - that was twelve years ago, now. Twelve years! Maybe another forty or so years left – barring tornado or fire or loggers?

Perhaps some kid will come up here and see it forty years from now. I wonder what he'll think. I wonder what his world will be like? I wonder if people will be happier with all the great advances that will have been made? I wonder if boys will still be killing themselves.

I hope people are happier forty years down the road. I'm worried, though, that there may just be more stuff to fight over - more wars and killing and hating – more greed – that's what's probably going to do in humanity in the end. My, I've become pessimistic - but then, I guess by definition, one who commits suicide is, at best, at least a little pessimistic, isn't he! (faint smile) I've never used those words in my mind before - commit suicide. It's Latin, you know, Di. From the words, sui meaning of oneself and the word *caedere*, meaning to kill. A truly terrible concept, isn't it?

I used to be so optimistic, Di. I knew everything would work out for the best - everything would be okay. Good would conquer evil. I'd grow up to be handsome instead of just ordinary. I'd marry a wonderful, beautiful girl and live happily ever after, raising a wonderful, beautiful family.

I guess that dream wore out a long time before I let myself realize it. I kept buying into all the wonderful things people kept telling me about myself. I fooled myself into thinking all that would one day make everything just fine - "hunky-dory," as Mom would say. Well, Di, it didn't. It just didn't all come together right. Perhaps I just had too much. Do you suppose? So smart I couldn't stay with my friends in school. So athletic I had to travel hundreds of miles to find any competition. So popular, everyone knew me and liked me, but, at the same time, disliked me (I believe) because I was just that popular and well liked. Crazy? I don't get it!

The storekeepers all wanted me to work for them, because I was such a good and dependable worker. So, I got all the best jobs - that meant other kids, of course, didn't! (How could they like me for that?) The kids all envied my good relationship with Mom and Pop - so much that they spent time at my place enjoying my parents. Sometimes, it seemed, I never got to have any private time with Mom and Pop at all.

I really think if I had been able to lose or fail more often, I'd have been a whole lot better off. It would have been like that shot, like an inoculation that would have helped me learn how to handle the little mistakes and disappointments, so when these big ones arrived, I'd have been more ready for them. More practiced in handling my problems. Does that make any sense, Di? Any sense at all?

If I were to raise a child, I'd sure let him fight his own battles and handle his own challenges. I'd help him pick up the pieces after a problem, but I'd let him prove to himself how failing and making mistakes were all okay - things he really could learn to handle by himself - let him practice, practice, practice!!!

My problem was that I just didn't ever meet problems I couldn't handle, so I couldn't get that kind of practice - that shot! That was just built into me, I guess - a built-in problem that didn't come to a head until this time in my life - like a bomb all wrapped up as a beautiful childhood gift, secretly rigged to explode when I reached 16.

Up above, I said problems I couldn't handle. I think I should have said, didn't handle. I always handled them, but maybe not in really appropriate ways. Somehow, I grew up feeling very different and, more than that, feeling it was bad to be different in those ways. If I could have only bought into Mom's idea that different was wonderful! I'm just beginning to see what she meant, but up till now it made no sense at all. "Too little, too late," as they say in dime novels.

Being the littlest, and therefore the cutest in your class,

didn't ever seem wonderful - it seemed terrible. To be so smart that everyone called you "Brains" may have been wonderful, but it always came across as a put down to me. What I was, what I had no choice about (being so damn smart) was a curse - anything but wonderful to me.

Then, I went through that period where I'd pull little pranks on people - teachers, parents, even Principal Kelley. Some of them were downright destructive - almost vicious. I wanted SO to really get it - to have to stay after school, get some swats, have Mom and Pop be called to school. Then I'd surely be one of the regular guys! Oh, how I wanted someone to just ask me why I was doing all those things. No one ever did! They all just smiled and referred to the episodes as, "Craig's clever little game." Clever? I was desperate and no one could see it! Well, no one except Ginny, of course. But she was just a kid. What could she do! Plenty, as it turned out! She ranted and raved at me and saw to it that I put a stop to all that nonsense!

Remember my awful complexion when I was fourteen. Some days, I could hardly get myself to leave the house. It was just a horrible time in my life! Pimples! Black heads! Red blotches where I'd pop the pimples, thinking that was somehow less offensive looking! I'd secretly wash my face with Cuticura soap. I'd bathe it in alcohol. I even washed it in urine after hearing that might help. It was just such a terrible, terrible, time. The silent anguish I felt, but no one around me seemed to understand why I was so out of sorts - so down and blue! (I guess I never offered to tell them, though, did I! Were they just supposed to guess? Interesting! It seems I did think it was up to them to take the initiative – now THAT was *really stupid*. I should have shared my despair.)

Now, I realize that I always thought I looked much worse than anyone else thought I did. And even if I had looked every bit as bad as I imagined, no one else would really have been bothered by it. Kids that age just have complexion problems. Some worse than others of course, but, as terrible as it seems, it just goes with the territory. All teens know that adults certainly don't judge a youngster's worth by his complexion. My friends didn't either, of course. Who was I so afraid of, then? I thought the girls wouldn't like me, didn't I!

Did the girls ignore me or run screaming down the street, covering their eyes when I approached them? No! But I certainly lived my life as if they did! It certainly isn't fair that pimples have to form just at the very time in life when our feelings about ourselves are so fragile.

I've decided every pimple on every teenager, has a direct line to their social judgment center in the brain, and sends these outrageous, inappropriate, and self-defeating messages down deep inside us! (I can smile about it now, but I know I never could have, then.)

Looks count for so little. If we could only come to understand that at 13 instead of at 33! Mother Nature certainly erred when she arranged it in that order, didn't she, Di! (sad, though finally pimple-free, face)
8:00 PM, July 5, 1952
4 hours to live

Dear Diary,
This won't be an easy hour, Di. I have to write that final letter to Ginny.

Dearest Ginny,
What does one say to a best friend at a time like this? I do not remember life without you, Ginny. You have just always been that solid, levelheaded, fun-filled person next to me. There has never been anything I could not talk to you about. (Well, except this one thing.) I hope you have felt that I have been there for you in this same way. I have tried.

We may be the only two people in town who really know all of each other's deep, dark secrets. (We are most certainly the only two who know, who put that cow up in the bell tower at the college! I still don't believe we did that! The poor cow! They had to shoot her to get her down!)

I know we had always planned to save the World together, Ginny. I guess the World will just have to depend on you. now. There is this one secret I haven't shared. If things go according to my plans, (and they always do, don't they!), by the time you receive this letter, I will have died. It was my own choice - done the way I wanted to do it, at the time I wanted to do it. Please try to be happy for me, even though, I know, you'll need to be sad for yourself.

I know I can't take your hurt away, and I am truly sorry that I placed it there. Don't feel guilty - you could not have done a single thing to change my mind. You have always been my rock. But you know me - if I can't do it perfectly, I will not do it at all. I cannot live the perfect life that everyone else expects me to live, so I just cannot live it at all.

I know, that makes no sense to you, now. The only important thing, right now, is that it does to me.

I have been thinking a lot about all these feelings I have for the important people in my life. It seems to me there must be several different kinds of love, Ginny. I love Mom in one very special way, John and Billy in another, and you in a very, very special way. Then, of course, all those different times when I "fell in love" with all those different girls! (I think that was "falling in lust" really. Those feelings were great - just not love, I think.) Fortunately, there is no special girlfriend to hurt right now.

But, back to you, Ginny. I find it hard to think of myself without you. I know you will do fine - after a while. I am not kidding myself. I know I am about to hurt those I love the most, in the worst of all possible ways. I am truly sorry about that. But I am so full of hurt myself, that I just can not be altruistic and understanding at this point. I have had to be those ways all of my life. This time it's for me.

You know that I do not believe in life after death, the way you do, Ginny. But, who knows, by the time you are reading this, I may just be the most surprised little angel that ever sprouted wings, sitting there barefoot on the edge of a nice white, fluffy cloud smiling down at you. If I am surprised that way, know that I will protect you always, if that is within my power.

Just don't count on it! (smile) I am convinced death is death, and once it comes, everything is over for ever - all the pain - all the despair - all the anguish - all the uncertainties - all of them, gone forever. I know what you are thinking! It also means the end of all of the happiness, all the accomplishments, all the fun, all the physical pleasures, all the friendships, all the chances to help others. They no longer balance out for me, Ginny.

You know I have really tried, these last twelve months. I really have! Every morning I have told myself that things will be okay. But by bedtime, things have not been Okay. Not for me. I spend my days doing those things that everyone else expects me to do - being just great at everything - making everyone else happy and proud - taking care of everyone from the tramps out at the trestle, to our "glorious mayor." I just can't do that anymore. It is just too hard to have to never, ever disappoint anyone - to always be there for everybody! If I had just been average - that would have been so grand - that, to me, would be heaven.

Well, you follow your dreams, Ginny. Mark is a fine person and great for you right now. Maybe he will be great for you later on too - maybe not. Either way, you will end up with someone just right for you. I know you will. I do have to wonder, if things had turned out differently, if you and I would/could have remained such good friends forever - I would hope so, but realistically, a man and a woman, each married to someone else, just do not remain best friends, do they. That is sad to think about, so I won't.

I am rambling. I guess I just hate to end this letter because that will mean good-bye in such a final way.

...Believe it or not, I am at a loss for words. Be happy! Be loved! Be Ginny!

From a lifetime of my love,

"Craigy"

PS: I really have no right to ask this, I know, but please help Mom through the next few months. She, too, loves you so!

Well, Di, it's written. I think I said what I wanted to say. Ginny will know what I wanted to say, anyway.

9:00 PM, July 5, 1952
3 hours to live

Dear Diary,

Here's what I wrote to Billy and John, my two best 'guy friends' in the whole World, Di.

Dear Billy and John,

I don't ask you to understand what I have done. It was solely my doing and you guys had nothing to do with it - no control over it whatsoever - so do not feel bad for me. I know it is the chicken's way out - We talked about that, didn't we. Well, cock-a-doodle-do!

I want - need - to thank you both for being such good and steadfast friends to have grown up with. (Miss Pierce would choke on that sentence, wouldn't she?) Can't you just hear her: "Mr. Franklin, I am deeply disappointed in the way you constructed the fourth sentence in the second paragraph on page three of this essay." Somehow, when she was passing back papers and spewing her running commentary on each student's errors, she seemed nine feet tall. And those glasses of hers that she'd look over - pardon me - "over which she would look" - Anyway, they seemed as big as saucers. Did you ever notice that? ("Is that something you ever noticed?" I give up!)

We had a good life together, didn't we! We learned so much from one another. My best memories are those hundreds and hundreds of hours we spent every summer, swimming under the railroad trestle in our swimming hole. We made it into a great place to swim and have fun, didn't we! Remember the summer when we were eight, and we built the dam to deepen it. It's no real miracle that it is still standing, either! We planned it well. We built it carefully. I did notice the other day that the railroad ties we used to make the spillway over the top are about rotted away. You may want to replace those this summer or the dam will start to wash out. That would be a shame - so many little guys still enjoy that spot.

You guys always just treated me like one of you - just another guy - just somebody your own age. Even after I started skipping grades and getting way ahead in school, I could always count on you two to just ignore all that. There is no way I can express to you how much that has meant to me. It was one of the very few places in my life where I wasn't treated like some sort of freaky super-brain. I love you both so much for that. I often wondered how you really felt about all the attention I got. It must have been Okay, huh? Thanks!

I know we've never come right out and asked much of one another. We were just always automatically there when one of us needed something. Well, I can't be there for you anymore, so I probably don't have the right to ask this, but I'm obviously going to anyway! Stop in and see Mom whenever you can. She loves you guys, and now with both Pop and me gone, she'll need you. Also, if you can, see that the little kids keep dropping in on Mrs. Stevens. She'll need more and more help now that she's getting so old. Eat one of her sugar cookies for me, now and then - Okay?

And, one final request - it's Really important to me. On Decoration Days, will you put a few flowers on my natural parent's graves and a few for Hanley. They won't have anyone left, now, to take care of them. Nothing special, just a few - Mrs. Stevens always lets me pick some of hers. Thanks. Seems like I've always been in your debt - Guess then, it's only fitting to stick it to you one more time!

You guys take good care of one another. I know you'll keep an eye on Ginny. She'll do Okay. She has Mark. He's a great guy. They'll make it, fine.

One last point I need to make, guys. I took one whole year to consider this final action of mine. One whole year! It wasn't just a whim or a temporary depression. I did everything in my power to avoid it. What I'm saying is, don't do anything dumb now, yourselves. YOU HEAR ME ! ! To have to die at 17 is rotten. DON'T FORGET THAT! IT'S ROTTEN ! !

A friend who loves you both dearly,

"Craigy"

It takes a lot of tears to write a letter like that, Di. An awfully lot of tears. ... Now, on to Doc.

Dear Doc,

I guess you already know everything I have to say to you - you always read me like a book. I want to try and say some things to you anyway.

Thanks for always being there for me - day and night, winter and summer, year after year - when sick, when happy, when proud, when blue. (Sounds almost like wedding vows, doesn't it!) I've known there was no way to repay you directly, just as I've known you wouldn't have wanted me to. I've tried to do those same kinds of things for some of the little kids and the older folks here in town - those same things that you did for me. You always talked of spreading kindness and caring around. I have tried to spread my share. You were right, of course! Nothing makes one feel so good as making someone else happier or more secure or better off in some little way.

By the way, I found out that you are the 'anonymous person' who provided my scholarship to college. I hope my knowing, doesn't take away any of the pleasure for you. Knowing that it was you, thrilled me beyond any words I can find to write here.

Remember our "birds and bees" talk when I was seven. I marched into your office after hours one night, and announced - demanded, I guess - that I wanted to cut to the quick on this "how do babies get here stuff." I'd received the run around from Pop and Parson and even Arnie. Now, I wanted the facts! I'll never forget the wonderful expression on your face, when, after you had finished - shown me pictures in your books and answered all my many questions - I responded to it all with, "That's really disgusting!"

I went right outside and spit. I'm not sure why but spitting seemed the thing to do. I couldn't imagine grown-ups doing such revolting things with each other. I spit ALL the way home. It helped! (By the way, I no longer spit at the idea.)

I remember the far more personal repeat of that talk, when I was 14. By then, of course, it was no longer disgusting - it was a totally fascinating, all consuming, fire-breathing passion. Thanks, Doc, for both chats - the first one that I demanded, and the second that you demanded!

Take care of yourself - I won't be around to gripe at you about wearing your boots in the winter or using an umbrella in the rain. Don't forget to take time to put up your storm windows in October - Billy will help you, I'm sure.

Please take care of Perry. Now that I'm not underfoot anymore, you'll probably have time for him. 'Raise' him well - like you did me, Doc. He has an inner strength and love for life I seem to have lost. Help him hold onto it. See that he gets the enclosed letter. Help him read it. Try to answer his questions. When he finally understands, you'll have no doubt - just watch his forehead. When it smooths out, you've succeeded! Truthfully, I suppose, it won't smooth out again for a long, long time now, will it?

Again, take care of yourself, Doc. I've been so very fortunate to have known you - for having you as a friend. Thanks for yelling at me when I needed it. Thanks for holding me close when I needed that. Thanks for always demanding integrity. I have loved you so, Dear Doctor.

Your most impatient little patient and loving friend,

Craig

PS: You know, Doc, you were the only one who ALWAYS called me Craig - not "Craigy." That made me feel SO grown-up - like you recognized me as a real person - not a 'diminutive' form of a person. Thanks for that, too

This is the letter I wrote to little Perry. He is six, Di. Not too bright, very poor and mostly unsupervised, but just brimming over with love and trust and caring. Our last time together was last night when we worked on the sandcastle. I guess I've sort of adopted him these past three years. A tough letter to write. How can I make him understand? I can't, of course. How can I at least help him through this? Through life?

Dear Perry,

I am writing you this letter because, in the whole wide World, you have been one of my very favorite people. I love your giggle. I love your innocence (you'll learn what that means later on). I love your expressive young face, your ruffled hair. I love that special look that breaks across your face when I'm explaining something to you - then I know that you understand. I have loved all our wrestling matches, our walks at the creek, our swims together, the tree climbing. You know all the things I mean.

I have loved helping you learn to read and to add and subtract. (And I loved all the excuses you could concoct for not beginning the lessons!) I've loved what a good worker you are, how trustworthy you are. I've loved how you really care about other people and try to help them out. I've loved the way you always minded me and did what I asked, even when you weren't sure why - you trusted me, and that's the greatest complement one person can pay another. I've loved all the talks we have had - especially about how you seem to understand that your Mom is doing the best she can, and how you need to be extra patient with her and help her out the best you can.

I've loved the way you love yourself just as you are. Never, never, forget to love yourself - just as you are, Perry. That's the thing about you I've admired the most. I've even been a little jealous of you for that, Perry, because I couldn't learn how to love myself that same way. You can do something I can't, and that is wonderful for you. I am very proud of you for that!

I don't know what life will bring for you, Perry. The people in this town really like you. It may be a good place for you to live and work and help, and to just be your very nice self. Remember, always do what YOU think is right - when you don't know for sure, talk to Doc or Parson. They'll always help you. Doc has been my best grown-up friend, here in town, ever since I was about your age - I know he'll be pleased to be yours, too, now.

There is no way you can understand why I had to go away and leave you like I did. I don't ask your forgiveness for that. I just ask that you always DO remember, if you will, the great times we have had together and all the things we have talked about. Never forget how to be the really nice person you are, and never, NEVER, forget how very much I have loved you, little buddy.

Forever, your "Big Buddy,"

Craigy

Di, I think that letter to Perry, may be the best piece I have ever written. I certainly hope that it is. (It absolutely needs to be.)

... You would think I'd be tired - beat - but the closer my time comes, the more I seem to be getting revved-up! I'm glad it is that way, Di!

10:00 PM, July 5, 1952

2 hours until I'm at peace

Dear Diary,

And now, the last of so many difficult letters I have had to write.

My Dearest Mom,

Of all the people on this Earth, you are the one, Mom, I never, ever, wanted to hurt, and I know I have now hurt you worst of all. Believe me, I tried everything I knew to avoid this. I spent an entire year trying to work things out. What I am trying to say, is that it was not an impulsive act, but, then, you know me well enough to know I haven't done anything impulsively for ten years.

I guess that is a part of my problem. A planned-out life is no fun - there is no adventure - no mystery left - no suspense. I have never been able to wonder, "How will I do?" I have always just done the best. How boring that must have been for everyone - it certainly was for me! And how unfair for all the other kids.

Sarah said it best once, when we were about ten. She said she was glad I kept skipping grades because then, she finally had her chance to shine. The further ahead (away) I got, the easier life became for her. I think she probably spoke the feelings of many of the kids. They never got credit for doing what was their best, so long as I was around doing what was my best.

I have always been puzzled by why they all continued to treat me so well. I often wondered what they said and how they really felt when I was not there - behind my back.

None of that is really new to you, I know. We talked about it so often, didn't we! Your advice was always the best - "Go ahead and do your best, but don't get a big head. Treat everyone as your equal. Go out of your way to be nice and helpful to everyone."

I did all those things, every day, Mom. But I was the only kid in town who had to be that way. So, even in trying to keep my friends from thinking of me as a freak, I had to do other things that made me feel like another kind of freak - a nice freak, a neat-freak, a let-me-help-you-freak.

My thoughts weren't always so pure, I'm afraid. That was my only truly private realm. In my fantasies, I could tell off my teachers and plant smoke bombs in the principal's office. I used to fantasize about getting a "B" (or even a "C") on a paper in school, just to see the reaction on everyone else's face.

Most of my dreams for myself, weren't anyone else's dreams for me. Parson always talked about my gifts, and how it was my responsibility to use them to benefit mankind (and, of course, he'd always add, "And for the Glory of God!"). I guess I bought into the, "helping mankind' part - hook, line and sinker! Can you understand how overwhelming that is - to think of living another 50 or 60 years and, day in, day out, taking care of everybody? Yes, you probably can. That's all you seem to have ever done, Mom - Me, Pop, everybody. HOW, Mom? HOW?

I'm sorry your own son died as an infant. He would have grown to love you so. I never felt I was quite worthy of being as precious to you as he would have been. I know that is not how you and Pop felt at all - you never indicated anything like that to me - but you know my head. It spins things at a wild rate!

I have really tried to be a good son. You know, that in my head, you are my only Mom! I have loved you so much! We have been so close. I felt so sorry for those kids who didn't feel close to their parents. That has been hard to understand. Sad, really.

I have wondered if we were closer, perhaps, because we found each other, rather than having been born to each other. I think that made you and Pop more precious to me - once I was old enough to think it through. You chose me first, but, Mom, I chose you too, later on when I could understand.

When I was small, I often wondered why you just took me in to raise. I wasn't a relative. I was just the new little kid in town who happened to move in next door - a smudged-faced, over-active, into everything, never satisfied, little kid, who wouldn't mind, and cried for three months straight after his own - no - his first family died.

As I grew older, it was no longer a mystery, because I had grown to know you - a wonderfully kind, giving, caring, sympathetic human being. You have given me everything and have raised me well, Mom. I hope I have helped fill a void for you.

Just a little last-minute business, here, Mom. Please don't bury me in a suit and tie. That's not me! How about a sweater - the blue and brown one you like so much. I'll bow to a white shirt if you want. Be sure to wrap me in my flag like you promised. That is really important to me. That way, I'll be taking a part of my heritage and a part of you, Mom, along with me. Enough of that.

This problem I've had, these past two years or so, was born into me, I think - nothing you or Pop are in any way responsible for - certainly nothing you could have ever prevented. It is, in fact, because of you, your love and understanding and caring, that I have been able to last this long.

Don't feel guilty. Only be proud - proud of yourself and Pop, and proud of the really nice kid you raised. I helped a lot of folks in my short life - more than many folks do even after living to a ripe old age. That was all possible because of your loving model, Mom.

I have loved you so very much. Good-bye now, my dear, dear, dear, Mom Franklin.

Your loving and obedient son,

Craig Lee Franklin, July 5, 1952

11:00 PM, July 5, 1952
1 hour from eternity

Dear Diary,

Happy Birthday To Craig! At last, I'm officially 17 years old!! Somehow, I still feel about 10!

I just took one last dip in the swimming hole, here under the railroad trestle, Di. I'll write as I just sit here in the warm night air and dry off. Nothing makes me appreciate the wonders of my body like swimming. Every square inch of my skin is feeling pressure on it, feeling movement, feeling a constant temperature everywhere all at the same instant. I'm weightless, in the water. No longer an object to be bound by or overpowered by gravity. Just me - my body - my thoughts - there alone! Submerge my head and even the sounds of the World disappear for a few wonder-filled moments. I can feel my blood and hear it rushing through my head. I close my eyes and see such beautiful colors flashing and shooting across my view! My hair floats effortlessly above my head. I feel each strand gently tugging at my scalp as if to say, "Here I am! I'm a part of you, Craig."

Tonight, brings back so many fine memories of being out here with John and Billy and others from time to time. Of building the dam. Of the talks we had about our changing bodies at 12 and 13 - recognizing and realizing that what was going on with my body must be okay, since it was also, obviously, going on with my friend's bodies as well. Those times we'd see who could run the fastest when we were 6, spit the farthest when 7, make another body 'cry Uncle' at 9, see who could pee the furthest up the tree trunk at age 10.

Being a guy has been SO wonderful. I can't even imagine being a girl. I suppose girls feel the same way, though - I mean, that for them, being a girl is the greatest. I hope they do. We sure treat them like lower level citizens sometime, don't we, Di. I suppose - I hope - that will change in time. (It will if Mom and Ginny have anything to say about it!) (smile)

Sitting here in the moonlight, I am suddenly seeing all the scars I have accumulated on my body over these seventeen years. Being still a bit wet, they glisten like little trails of white icing in the moonlight. My knees must have a half dozen scars each - those mostly happened before I was seven, I'd say. I surely was an active little go-getter in those days. Poor Mom! Poor teachers!! Poor principal Kelley!!! I guess I wasn't afraid to try anything, back then. (Was I too dumb to be afraid, or was I too smart to be afraid - I wonder?)

Here's the scar on my right foot where I stepped on that broken bottle at swimming camp, and these two long ones, on my left wrist, where my wet hand slipped off the window latch and crashed through the glass - sixteen stitches, if I remember correctly! If Doc had a dollar for every stitch he's put into this body, he could retire. (smile)

I have a list here of things I want to be sure to do during these last few minutes, Di. (Thoughtful pause ...) I can't even just kill myself without being organized and neat about it! ... Okay, well, that is who I have been, isn't it – 'plan ahead, neat, level-headed, friendly, don't ever hurt anybody Craig.'

Di, did you know that when you die, your bladder empties automatically because the sphincter muscles relax? So, excuse me a minute while I go over beyond the other trees and urinate. I don't want anyone to find me here in a pool of my own stinking urine! ...

... While I was gone, I also folded up all my clothes and put them in a nice neat, 'Craig-like' pile here beside me. I'll try to tuck you safely inside them when I'm nearly finished here, Di.

Di, you know me – 'always over-prepared, Craig' - Well, you'll get a charge out of this! I brought a blanket along tonight so whoever finds me will have something with which to cover me. Can you believe I really did that? A dead body seems to give most folks the creeps, so they hurry up and cover it - head to toe - but especially the head. Strange! It's Okay to look at the corpse once it's all laid out in the casket, but not before. People (social customs, really, I guess) are SO strange!

I remember wanting to be there at the mortuary when they prepared Pop's body. He would have approved of that. I thought that then, of all times, someone who loved him, not just a couple of strangers, should be there with him as he was being made ready for his eternal rest. It's no surprise, I suppose, that everybody thought I was some kind of ghoulish pervert!

Well, Di, I guess this is it. The time has finally arrived. I'm going to take the pills now. It should only take a few minutes - ten or fifteen – maybe twenty. I could have selected cyanide or something that works immediately, but, like Socrates, I want to experience the process of dying. One last new thing to learn about!

...There. The deed is done. I feel a real sense of relief. It's a good decision, I believe. I have often wondered how I'd feel about all this once it had been done. It truly seems correct ... Quite terrible, but correct.

The moon is so bright tonight, Di. That's nice. I can sit here against the tree and see to write. I can watch the moon beams dancing over the water ... I just skipped a stone across the pond. It was like fireworks, only all white and silver. Like sparks sailing here and there - ever widening, glistening rings in the water - fainter and fainter and now gone - so smooth again. Like a mirror now. Watching the water seems to be hypnotic tonight, or maybe ...

I've always loved falling asleep, Di. That brief period between being fully awake and finally asleep. I'm always intrigued by the images and strange new ideas that dance in and out of my mind, then. That's how it is becoming now, Di... Images and thoughts - Mom's face, Pop in his casket, the time Harley bloodied my nose, Parson standing in the pulpit, crying on Ginny's shoulder a few days ago, - Dear Ginny, I do love you so, good friend - falling off my bike while coasting down Hellman's Hill, swimming training laps, kissing Mary Jane (Boy, can Mary Jane ever kiss!!!), trapping with Arnie. ... My mouth is so dry I can't think - that should be 'speak', shouldn't it. Well, tonight it's 'think'! It seems chilly. ...I'm crying - Why am I crying? I'm so happy at last - so really, really happy at last! When was the last time I was this comfortable, this at peace with myself, this free from fears and cares, this is just-the-way-I-want-ME-to-be? I feel so lite - its good too feal - that way I no Im still hear. My writing is becomming so poor now, but youll know what it says, wont you di.

My dear Di, I guess its just about that time. Time to close you for the last time. time to finally say good-by to you, old friend. I do hope that with each volume, Ive left you a bit wiser than befor. Thank you for being so patient with me, Di! For listening so long and well. And thanks Di, for helping me see my mistakes. It seemed so often that only after Id put down some great plan or thought here on your pages that I could clearly see how poor it was. Thanks for reflecting the truth for pointing out errant pathways   for clearing my muddled mind. Thanks for accepting anything I had to say - anyway I felt - without question, without censorship.   Thanks for absorbing what must have become gallons of tears over the years - tears, which as I'd write, would stream down my cheeks as they are, in fact doing right now. I wonder why? They'd fall onto your pages and blur things beyond recognition. Don't do that now, tears. Please.   Until now, Di, you have just patiently taken and taken and taken. Perhaps someday, if these pages are ever perused by others it will finally become your turn to give.   Please do give freely of these words to anyone who wishs to consider them. but let the readers be warned - These have been My thoughts -My interpretations and My words - based on my experiences.... They will never exactly fit anyone else.   DEATH AT 17 IS ROTTON!!!... Goodby my dear Dear Di, and good-bye to all that I have loved

Epilogue One
One year to the hour, later

11:00 PM, July 5, **1953**

Dear Diary, I'm back!

Happy Birthday To Craig! I'm officially 18 now. I feel about 110.

What a year this has been, Di! The year in which I killed myself and lived to tell about it! Not many guys can boast that, now, can they? (faint smile)

I really had successfully killed myself, you know, Di. I had done everything just right. Everything I could plan had been carefully taken care of. Who could have known that on that particular night, at that particular time, there under that particular railroad trestle, that particular old tramp would happen by?

They tell me he carried me over his shoulder the whole mile and a half back to town. A little, toothless, unshaven scruff of a man, Doc said. He rang Doc's bell, handed me over into Doc's arms, and left without so much as a word. No one remembers ever having seen him before. We have never seen him since.

I guess I'm back out here under the trestle by the swimming hole tonight, hoping he'll 'return to the scene' one year later (and all that dramatic kind of thing).

Tonight, I truly love him for what he did. I'd like so much, to be able to tell him that - face to face. For months afterwards, however, I hated him and his interference with (as Parson puts it), "the Devil's own passion."

I wonder why he did it – spoiled my plan - that little tramp man? He didn't know me. He probably couldn't even tell for sure, if I were alive or dead. Why didn't he stick around Springfield - at least long enough to see if I were going to be okay? Perhaps he was a wanted man and couldn't risk anyone recognizing him. Perhaps he was telling me, even the life of a tramp is better than an all too early death. Perhaps he had lost a son of his own - or never had known the joy of having had one. You have one now, Mr. Tramp, Sir! You gave me my life! I'll gladly be your son.

Arnie used to tell me that a gift is not the truest gift of love, unless it's given anonymously. I think he meant that when you take credit for giving it, you're garnering part of the spotlight for yourself - detracting from the selfless aspect of giving, by taking credit. It's as if you are giving a gift in order to receive recognition for having done so - like buying attention, if not also, obligation and appreciation and perhaps even, love.

Well, Mr. Tramp, by this measure, your gift to me was, indeed, the truest gift of love. I do hope that deep in your heart you know that, Sir.

They tell me it was 5:00 AM on July 7th when my eyes finally fluttered open. I'd been in a coma, there in Doc's own bed, for about 30 hours. He and Mom had been there with me the whole time, I guess. Ginny had just come to give Mom a break, and it was Ginny's face I saw first, as I blinked open my heavy, aching eye lids against the hurtful light.

For ever so short a moment, with the light of dawn breaking in the window behind her head, it appeared as if she were an angel, and that - surprise! surprise! - I'd gone to heaven. (If this were heaven, I'd surely gone through a lot of unnecessary trouble to get here!) (smile) Undoubtedly, that question of Heaven had been weighing on my mind as I had slipped away earlier.

But then, gradually at first, it all began coming back to me. A flash here - a flash there - I knew where I was - Doc and I had spent so many hours together talking about life right there in that same room. And Ginny - no better face in the whole

World to greet me!

Presently - quite soon, in fact - the realization that I was still alive set in. I felt suddenly desperate! Suddenly angry - SO VERY ANGRY!!!! "God damn it," I screamed! (A most uncharacteristic response from one Craig Franklin, the original nice boy.)

I remember how I began sobbing uncontrollably and beating on the pillow with my fists and upper arms. Ginny sat on the bed beside me and, instinctively, I guess, took my head in her lap. At first, I resisted, but soon gave in. She just silently held me close - the very way Mom had done so many times before. She gently rocked me back and forth letting me rant and rave and cry myself back to life.

After a while - no idea how long - I realized I was just quietly sobbing. Ginny was patting my tear-drenched face with her handkerchief. I knew it was hers - it had the smell of her lilac perfume.

I looked up into her strong, half-smiling face. She brushed back my hair. "How's Mom doing?" I asked in a broken whisper.

"Better than you might expect," she said softly. "Shall I get her, now?"

"Not yet. What can I say to her? ... Where is she?"

"She's been here the whole time. I came in about a half hour ago so she could get some rest. Billy took her home. Doc said he'd let her know the minute there was a change."

"They let her stay in town all night?"

I remained confused about many things.

Ginny nodded yes and smiled, letting it go. I just lay there quietly for a while longer. "What time - what day is it," I asked?

"You've been a coma for over thirty hours, Craig. Doc literally brought you back to life."

I closed my eyes ever so tightly and cried some more.... Then, Doc came in.

"Well, it's about time, young man! I DO have other patients, you know!"

Good old Doc! Calm, cool, collected and ever smiling - standing there over me, taking my pulse with his strong, steady, reassuring hand; gently pulling back my eyelids one at a time; patting me on the shoulder.

"Anyone special you want right now, Craig?"

"No, just Ginny right now, I guess. Better let Mom know, I suppose."

"I'll be back in a little while, then." At the door, he turned back toward me. "It's really good to have you back with us, Craig. I hope someday soon you can also be happy about that." He paused. "Billy and John are out front. May I tell them you're okay?"

"Billy and John? Yeah, I guess so. Boy, what a mess, huh, Doc?"

"You've always been good at cleaning up messes, Craig. The only difference is that this time, the mess is yours, instead of somebody else's. Time heals, and we'll all be here to help - when you're ready for us."

He left and closed the door.

I reached for Ginny's hand and held it tightly against my chest! I couldn't remember ever having held her hand before - well, not since we were little kids and that was mostly just so we wouldn't get separated from each other. I really needed to hold it just then - maybe for that same reason.

Suddenly, from outside the window, rose such a cheer as I'd never heard before. It was like a thousand voices cheering the winning field goal in the last second of the Big Game!

I looked up at Ginny, a question, undoubtedly, on my face.

"They've all been out there, just sitting on the lawn, ever since they heard about you," she said. They just began showing up - one or two at a time. Billy and John were first, I guess. Every kid in town is out there, and, I suppose, half the grown-up as well - all just waiting to hear. ... You know Parson, every once in a while, he offers a prayer."

I almost smiled at that. Good old Parson! He just wouldn't give up!

Presently, the cheering broke into wild applause - whistles, even!

"This thing has sure brought the town together, Craig. They all love you so much."

"Harley?" I asked, not even sure why.

"You'd never believe it, Craig, but Harley's been out there taking care of Perry all this time."

That brought to my face the first smile of my new life! The second, I'm afraid, wasn't to come for many, many weeks!

Needless to say, I recovered - begrudgingly, at first - but I recovered. I was a confused mixture of disappointment, desperation, rebellion and anger. I had changed. I was hard to live with. I was not a nice person by any measure.

Mom never asked why. No one did for a long time. Then, in late August, when he felt the time was right, patient old Doc finally confronted me one day there in his office. He removed his glasses and shook them at me like parent's finger at a wayward child.

"If you're going to spend the rest of your life hating yourself and everybody else in this World, a lot of us around here sure have wasted a bunch of valuable time on you! You've been so obnoxious this past month, I've felt like handing you a new bottle of pills and telling you to go do it right this time. For a genius, Craig, you can be so blasted dumb, sometimes!"

Talk about feeling rage! Oh, how I wanted to knock that old man across the room! ... Instead, I broke into tears and we stood there holding each other close and tight for ever so long.

"I'm just so afraid to live again."

"I know, I know," Doc reassured. "But you have no choice, now, do you? You have obviously decided not to do yourself in, or you'd have done it by now, wouldn't you? Let us in, Craig. It's no sin for Craig Franklin to need others to help him."

That phrase, "Let us in, Craig. It's no sin ... to need others...," turned my life around. I realized that I had grown up feeling so guilty because I had needed to take so much, from so many, for so long - as if it had, in fact, been a sin just to have been a helpless, needy, little orphan boy. I certainly couldn't ask for anything more.

Doc and I talked a lot after that. I'm really doing fine now - stronger than ever, I think. I am even learning to say "No" (well, once in a while, anyway!). (Smile) I have come to realize that living needs to be a two-way street - It's grand to need to help others, like I need to do, but we all need to allow others to help us, as well – it's good for us and for them.

I used to go around town helping out everybody - and, though I wasn't always consciously aware of it, making sure they knew I was the one doing the helping! I needed to see that they realized I was paying them back, you see. Not very selfless in Arnie's terms. Quite selfish in fact. They didn't expect to be paid back. I truly thought they did! Perhaps, the 'next time' I die, I'll have my tombstone inscribed with Doc's wonderful phrase - LET OTHERS IN!

In these last twelve months, I've also come to realize that it is okay - necessary, in fact - to take some selfish time every day - time just to do what Craig wants to do for himself. I have begun to understand what Arnie meant when he told me, "Today is *not* just practice for tomorrow - Today is your life, so LIVE it."

Well, through all of this, I have devised this personal philosophy for living, Di. It's not very complicated, but I sure had to go through years of turmoil and anguish finding it. For what it may be worth, here it is:

Every day I try to do four things:

1. I do those tasks required of me. (We all have jobs and responsibilities we must regularly fulfill, like it or not!)

2. I do something nice for someone else each day. (Something not expected or required - something extra. Sometimes it has to be done in an open and obvious way, but whenever possible, I do it anonymously. What an absolutely grand feeling that brings!)

3. I learn something new every day - something I didn't know the day before. (It makes me know I'm alive and growing. I may read a passage from an encyclopedia, memorize a Shakespearean sonnet, learn how to adjust a carburetor, how to 'Around the World' with Perry's yo-yo. Just something new! I also think minds die a rapid death when they aren't regularly exercised from the inside out - like, rather than just passively listening to a drama on the radio [outside-in], writing a drama for the radio! [inside-out].)

4. Finally, I do something, very selfishly, just for me. (I swim, run, write, read, listen to the radio, hang with friends, go on a date, invent, loaf. It renews me! It reaffirms to me that I am important, too!)

So far, it has been making a very well balanced and

satisfactory life, Di. I'm really happy. Really at peace. Each night at bedtime, when I know I've achieved each of these things that day, I sleep so well. I feel so contented, relaxed, so committed to life. If, on occasion, I've somehow missed one of them, it's no big deal. I know I can just catch up the next day.

This philosophy may not work for everyone, but I am convinced there is a philosophy out there that will work for everyone if they will just carefully and thoughtfully search for it. We each must actively *build* our life. We don't dare just sit around waiting for it to happen all by itself. We must each take control – set goals and work toward them. Ask our heroes what's most important in life to them.

It has been a wonderful year, and it has been a terrible year, Di. In December I got engaged to Mary Jane - I know, I'm way too young, too broke, too everything negative, but we decided that we were just too much in love not to commit to one another. We would wait three years to be married - I'd have finished my Ph.D. in Clinical Psychology by then, and she would be in her senior year in college.

On prom night, Mary Jane and two of her girl friends were killed in a car-train accident. Of course, I was devastated. But, with time, I am bouncing back. No one will ever replace her in my heart, but now I realize that my heart also has room for another love, whenever that may come along. I am being patient.

Like I said, it's been a wonderful year, and it's been a terrible year. In September, Mom told me she had cancer - She'd known for several months. She died six weeks later.

Remember, Di, that last supper that I had with Mom, before I did my 'terrible thing'. We felt so close. We shared so much. We felt one another's love so completely. I thought I was saying good-bye to her, because I'd soon be gone. Now, I realize that Mom thought she was saying good-bye to me, because she'd soon be gone. I miss her so much, Di, but all those memories we made together, will always be tucked away deep inside me, just waiting there for those times when I need or want them. Isn't that grand! Loved ones never really leave you!

It's been a wonderful year, and it's been a terrible year. I sold the house and moved into that room over the grocery store. I'll use the money from the house and from Mom to help with the university expenses in September. I've taken this past year off from school to put my brain back together. I've done a lot of writing, worked at the grocery, and Doc has had me helping him talk with kids who are in (or nearly in) trouble - kids who, for various reasons, are upset or just need to talk. Kids who are willing to take seriously Doc's motto, *"Let others in."*

That's how I think I want to spend my professional life, Di. Helping kids find themselves. It seems I've already had a lot of practice. Now that I am finally finding myself, I think I'll be very good at it, Di, don't you!

Ginny and Mark broke up. That was really hard on her. For a change, I have been able to be of help and support to her. She'll be starting college here in town in September. She wants to teach handicapped kids. She'll be so good at that. She too, has had a lifetime of practice - after all, she's really done a pretty good job on me, wouldn't you say, Di! She's been so much help to me – this year, especially. It's scary thinking about finally being separated from Ginny - her staying here in Springfield, and me going off to the university at Bloomington. If we just hadn't always been best friends, perhaps ...

Well, Di, it is late (early, really, I guess), and it appears I've drawn a no-show on my Mr. Tramp. I didn't really expect him to show up, of course. I suppose that was just an excuse to get myself back up her on this particular night and face myself as I am now - the brand new me – fully in love with the life I had decided to snuff out – now, unimaginably terrible!

So, good-bye little Craigy. You served me well! Despite your predicaments and problems, I can now, at last, really appreciate you, and understand how very much I do love you - right down to your bulging brain, your freaky freckles, and your sandy, mussed hair. (One definitely, full-fledged, world's broadest-ever, certifiably genuine, ear to ear, grin!)

I've been working on a special poem, Di. One that tries to convey the new me - the deep, deep down inside, new me.

Sunrise

Though sunset's beauty, won't deny,
I highly recommend
You start each day with eyes raised high -
Let sunrise greet you, friend!

At first, horizon's distant glow,
With random rays of light
That chase the shadows down below
As if to tease the night.

Soft bands of hues across the sky -
So tentative, at first -
That then explode, as if the dye
From painter's pots had burst!

I've found one never can be sure
When sunrise, dim, gives way,
But soon, that wondrous heav'nly blur
Submits to light of day.

Each sunrise promises, anew,
Another day is mine
In which to work and play and do
Those things that make life shine.

So, hope you'll take the time to view
The sunrise serenade.
I wish just splendid ones for you.
And hope they never fade!

   Happy Birthday to Me! I'm officially one day old today!
Somehow, I feel 18!! How absolutely g-r-a-n-d ! ! !

Epilogue Two:

65 years later (to the hour)
11:00 PM, July 5, 2017

Enjoying every day as it comes

Dear Diary,

Happy Birthday To Me! I'm officially into my 80s now. I still feel 18 (deep inside my graying head and wrinkled face, that is!)

This is a very special entry in my diary, friends, for it is to become a part of a book, which I hope will serve well, each new generation of young people, as they sort their way through the trials and wonders of adolescence.

Please understand, that from the moment I (that's Craig, of course) realized I had not died, that diary - so carefully planned for you to read, became a very private, infinitely personal document to me. It was written to be read and used by a World without young Craig. When I lived, its purpose seemed to have died. It has remained a totally private diary these sixty some years.

But seeing the difficult challenges and problems besetting young people today, and being so deeply troubled by the continuing rise in the suicide rate among our precious teenagers, I have decided to share it, with the hope that it has a timeless message to convey - a message of hope - a message of patience - a message about the joy of living and giving and accepting - a message about how this one teenage life, saved from a premature death, did, later on I believe, help change the World for the better.

This is a message about how *your* life, when played out over the normal ups and downs of living, can also, change and improve the World forever! Just how you are going to change the World, of course, we probably don't know yet! I hope *that*, by itself, makes the challenges of living an exciting, wonder-filled adventure - a life-long quest, which, day by day, you will pursue with zest and vigor and fascination! *"What wonderful, still unknown, things, am I going to be able to do for someone, today?"*

Now, my friends, it may appear as though there is a boastful tone to these last few pages of this book. I do not intend to boast here - just to bring you up to date on a life that could not have been, save for that nameless, selfless, toothless, unshaven, little scruff of a man, who, on that hot moonlit July night in 1952, allowed me a second chance at life.

Let's return to where the diary left us in the previous section. I went on to finish my Doctor's degree in clinical psychology as planned.

Ginny and I kept in surprisingly close contact after I went away to the university. I found myself going back to Springfield more and more often. One Saturday afternoon in February, Ginny and I were having a cup of coffee at that same little hometown cafe where we had talked so many times before. We were nineteen. Ginny sighed deeply, reached across the table taking my hands in hers, looked me straight in the eye and gently asked, "Well, are we going to get married, or what?"

Astounded and taken completely by surprise, I blurted out, "I don't want to marry anybody I know!" Yes, I know, it sounded dumb to me, too, when I heard it said out loud, but for years and years it had made such perfect sense, tucked away there inside my head.

A long silence followed. Then, Ginny began to giggle as only she could giggle. To my surprise, I found myself giggling right along with her. I pulled her clasped hands up to my lips and kissed them. We leaned in and let our foreheads touch. We looked into each other's faces - faces we'd both looked upon thousands of times before - but that time, we each saw someone brand new!

Now folks, bells did not peel out! Heavenly light did not encompass her lovely face! Cupid (for all the credit he gets) did not pierce our hearts with his fabled arrows of love. But I am here to tell you, something indescribable did happen there in those few moments!

The next thing I remember was standing up on my chair and yelling out for all to hear: "Ginny and I are getting married!" The folks who were gathered there - our life-long friends - all turned toward us and broke into applause! Al, the longtime cook, poked his head around the corner and yelled, "Well, it's about time!" Everyone nodded and laughed - someone whistled! It seems that I was the last person in town to realize that marrying Ginny was the best thing that could possibly happen to me. (I'll bet even you knew that many pages ago, didn't you!)

We were married in June. Parson tied the knot. Doc and Billy stood up with me. I so wished that John could have been there with us, too, but he had been a casualty of War. Rest in Peace, Good Friend.

A few years later, we had a son - we named him David Thomas Franklin - such a big name for such a tiny, red, helpless, wizened-up, new little human being. It didn't hit either Ginny or me until we sat there in the car, ready to leave the hospital parking lot. Franklin was asleep in her lap. We looked at one another, proud, but terrified - How in the World are we supposed to know how to raise this precious child?

Well, we did, and pretty well, I'd say. He became a wonderful human being - an author, a psychologist, an aviator, a community leader, and an all-round nice guy - always up to his heart in charity work.

Ginny taught children with learning problems and developed new and better materials and methods for other teachers to use. She would typically teach one semester at the university school each year, occupying the rest of her time as photographer, musician, homemaker, activist, friend to all, and as a wonderful mother and foster mother.

Although David was our only child, we cared for several dozen homeless children, over the years - some for just a few months, others for several years. To me, now, a house without young people just hardly seems like a home.

How did they turn out? We have, among our number, a Juilliard and a Harvard graduate, several successful tradesmen, a gigolo, and a perennial jailbird! Most are happy, successful adults now, busily tending to their own families. Interestingly, many of them have also taken in an occasional foster child. Several have adopted. Love and caring just grow and grow, once they are carefully planted and properly nurtured! Isn't that grand! Isn't that wonderful! Isn't that the very best part of *life*!

What about me? Well, with the exception of one, short, very dark period in my life, I have followed 'Craig's' four-point philosophy quite closely over these past sixty plus years. I've spent most of my life as an author – often ghost writing for other people - staying anonymous - helping others say what was on their minds. In and about it all, I've managed several dozen novels on my own – all based in positive social values – many written under pennames.

Throughout a large part of my professional career, I maintained a counseling practice - mostly for kids and their parents. This activity has brought me great pleasure and rewards, far beyond Craig's most vivid adolescent fantasies. I believe I have helped many hundreds of youngsters learn to love themselves and handle themselves and others in fruitful and self-fulfilling ways. I'm proud of that! I'm so pleased that I was *here* for them when they needed somebody. My many young friends and I thank you again, Mr. Tramp, Sir. I sometimes wonder what would have become of James or Winston or Paul or Jamal if young Craig had succeeded that night under the railroad trestle.

I have also had the pleasures of teaching grade and high school; being a college professor; being a gardener; doing medical research; building my own home; being a consultant to statesmen and TV networks, and to leaders of business and industry; serving on various national and international professional organizations; being a 'Big Brother'.

As a teenager, I had the mistaken idea that I had to decide

on just one thing I wanted to be or do for the rest of my life. You can be and do all sorts of things. Like Mom said, "There is so much to learn and do, and only one short lifetime in which to pursue it." I planted my 'base' in the world as a psychologist and then augmented it in a variety of fascinating and useful ways.

I hope you understand that I have related these things, not to sound important, but to emphasize that no one - not at ten or fourteen or sixteen or even at eighty - can possibly know ahead of time, just what important contributions he or she will make, or what opportunities and joys may be experienced, later on in life. I often say, with all sincerity, that I still don't know what I'm going to be when I grow up! A premature death cancels all hope that those things will ever happen – the brutally blunt truth is that a dead person can't save the world – or more importantly, help save his or her little part of it – or experience the wonderous joys his or her life can have in store. *Bad times pass.* Life continues to amaze and astound me. I fully expect that it always will.

Dear Friends, may I leave you with this thought. It is from a story that Craig wrote during that "wonderful and terrible" year when he was seventeen: A wise, old, mountain man, was passing on his best advice to a teen boy.

"Grow and learn from life's downside - it can make you strong and wise if you will just not give up. Revel and rejoice in life's upside - it brings you pleasures and rewards beyond belief! Never be content with considering just two sides to an issue - find two hundred sides if that's what it takes to create a satisfactory solution or understanding. There are always acceptable options if you learn to search wisely and tirelessly. Shamelessly, search out *help* if you need it – it is always available if you commit to life. Build a wonderful memory every day, and you will, indeed, be the wealthiest person who ever lived!"

May your life, with all its normal ups and downs, play out as a wonderful surprise to you, as you spread your caring spirit to touch – with love – those within your reach who need your special gifts.

Yours Truly,

Craig Franklin – the grown-up version,
BA, Bachelor of Arts
MS, Master of Science
PhD, Doctor or Philosophy
RHP, Really Happy Person

The End

[For a glance at how life had been for Craigy
in happier days as a
super-intelligent nine-year-old,
read,

And Then Came Arnie,

by Tom Gnagey.]

www.ingramcontent.com/pod-product-compliance
Lightning Source LLC
Chambersburg PA
CBHW020319290526
45785CB00007B/2848